English Engraved Silver

P over M, attributed to. 'The Prodigal Son Journeys into a Far Country'
PLATE, parcel-gilt, one of a set of twelve illustrating the parable
1568 hallmark. Goldsmith's mark *FR monogram*. D. 7½in (19 cm)
Collection of the late Duke of Buccleuch. See pages 37, 144

ENGLISH ENGRAVED SILVER
1150 to 1900

CHARLES OMAN

Faber & Faber

LONDON AND BOSTON

other books by the author

Caroline Silver 1625–1688
English Domestic Silver
English Church Plate
English Silver in the Kremlin
The Golden Age of Hispanic Silver
British Rings 800–1914

*First published in 1978
by Faber and Faber Limited
3 Queen Square London WC1N 3AU
Filmset and printed in Great Britain by
BAS Printers Limited
Over Wallop Hampshire*

British Library Cataloguing in Publication Data

Oman, Charles
 English engraved silver, 1500–1900.
 1. Silverware, English—History
 I. Title
 739.2'3'742   NK7143
 ISBN 0-571-10498-3

Foreword

So much has been written about English silver since interest in it was aroused in late Victorian times, that it is surprising that I was able to find an aspect of the subject which had been neglected. The names of the artists with whom I deal are not to be found in Arthur Grimwade's *London Goldsmiths 1697–1837: Their Marks and Lives*, nor in Sir Charles Jackson's *English Goldsmiths and their Marks*, since the engravers were not obliged to register marks. Jackson had little to say about them in his *Illustrated History of English Plate*, but E. Alfred Jones was showing a greater interest in them in his last years. I had noted this gap in our knowledge and contributed four articles in *Apollo* in 1957 (LXV, 173–6, 218–21; LXVI, 109–11). I continued my researches during the last twenty years and must record the help which I have received from those who, alerted by my articles, drew attention to interesting pieces which they had discovered. I must thank especially Mr. Arthur Grimwade, Mr. Thomas Lumley, Mr. Eric N. Shrubsole and Mr. C. J. Shrubsole.

In my archival research I have received much help from Miss Susan Hare, Librarian at Goldsmiths' Hall, whilst Miss Margaret Gill guided me through the Bewick papers in the Laing Art Gallery, Newcastle, and my former colleague at the Victoria and Albert Museum, Mrs. Shirley Bury, directed my attention to the places where I might obtain information about the engravers of the Victorian period. From the Metropolitan Museum, New York, I have received most valuable help from Miss Yvonne Hackenbroch and Miss Jessie McNab; and from Colonial Williamsburg, Virginia, from Mr. John D. Davis. I must thank also all those who have thrown scraps of information to me over the years.

Turning to the illustrations, I must acknowledge with sincere thanks the gracious permission of Her Majesty the Queen for permission to reproduce the pieces shown as Figures 65, 66, 70 and 115. I must also thank the following private owners: the late Duke of Buccleuch, the late Sir Montgomerie Fairfax-Lucy, Bart., the Lord Gisborough, the late Mrs. Ionides, the Earl of Lonsdale, the late Mr. C. Ruxton Love,

Foreword

Mrs. Elizabeth M. Miles, the Marquess of Ormonde, the late Earl of Stamford, and also others who prefer not to have their names recorded. For similar reasons I thank the following Cambridge colleges: Christ's, Emmanuel, Gonville and Caius, St. John's, Trinity Hall; these Oxford colleges: Corpus Christi, St. John's, Magdalen, New College; the following cathedrals: Canterbury, Ripon, Southwell, Worcester; numerous parish churches; the following corporate bodies: the Bank of England, the Barber Surgeons' Company, the Clothworkers' Company, the Goldsmiths' Company; the following museums and libraries: Ashmolean Museum, Oxford; Bodleian Library, Oxford; British Museum; Glasgow Museum and Art Gallery; Hermitage Museum, Leningrad; Jewish Museum; King's Lynn Museum; Laing Art Gallery, Newcastle-upon-Tyne; Metropolitan Museum, New York; National Army Museum; National Museum of Wales, Cardiff; Colonial Williamsburg, Virginia; Sterling and Francine Clark Institute, Williamstown, Mass.; the following firms: Bruce Corporation; Messrs. Christie, Manson and Wood; Hoare's Bank; Messrs. Thomas Lumley; Messrs. S. J. Shrubsole; Messrs. Sotheby; Messrs. Spink.

Putney, March, 1978   CHARLES OMAN

Contents

9

Illustrations

❦

Illustrations

Illustrations

13

Illustrations

Illustrations

15

Illustrations

Introduction and Definitions

Engraving is, of course, a very obvious means of decorating silver and was already in use in Anglo-Saxon times, so that the decision to begin the present study in the twelfth century is merely a matter of convenience since it avoids discussion of the small number of very early pieces.

The motives which have prompted the engraving of silver are few and fall into three main groups:

1. Recording ownership or donorship;
2. Recording a historical event or some religious subject;
3. Pure decoration.

On many pieces more than one of these motives are in evidence.

The artists who have engraved English silver have included many who had been born abroad. Some of these spent only a short time in this country but most of them seem to have settled for life. They came mainly from the Low Countries and from Germany and their presence was most apparent in the sixteenth and seventeenth centuries. French artists do not seem to have made much impression in this country until the close of the seventeenth century when some came partly as the result of the Revocation of the Edict of Nantes. They were of less artistic importance than the Huguenot goldsmiths who arrived at this time. This was due to the different artistic traditions of the two countries. French plate was more sculptural and afforded less scope for engraving. France produced fine engravers but they were employed mainly on small-scale work such as the decoration of watches. It seems to have taken even the most able of them, Simon Gribelin, some time to discover that there was a demand in England for finely engraved silver. Whilst the number of French engravers of plate who worked in England was never large, French engraved ornament was borrowed freely. Here we may emphasize that although plate was engraved in every country, it was only in the Low Countries, Britain and Germany (and to a lesser degree Scandinavia), that it can be said to have flourished. The relative importance of these countries varied at different times but in the first half of the eighteenth century the best work was being done in England.

The largest piece of engraved English silver is indubitably the plaque on the top of the table presented by the merchants of the City of London to William III (Figure 70). It measures 29 × 48 in (73·7 × 122 cm). The point at which the lower limit should be fixed is more of a problem. I have decided to include freedom- and tobacco-boxes but to exclude engraved medallions, flatware, watch-cases and all forms of jewellery.

I have dealt only with pieces which have been decorated with engraving which has not been filled in subsequently with niello or enamel. In engraving, metal is removed by the graver, in contrast to flat-chasing in which the lines are made by the pressure of the tools without the removal of any silver. It is frequently difficult to distinguish flat-chasing from engraving when linear effects are attempted, as in the large group of pieces decorated with chinoiserie in the latter part of the reign of Charles II. Pounced decoration is also excluded, whilst the use of etching which is found on German pieces made at the end of the sixteenth century did not spread to England at that time. A limited use of acid for giving a 'pickled' background was in use in Victorian times (Figure 148).

There appears to be no clear evidence as to how closely the flat-chasers were associated with the Goldsmiths but it would seem that some worked free-lance as did some of the engravers. Pounced decoration was probably always done in the goldsmith's workshop since it was used mainly to record ownership and could be obliterated more easily than engraving when the piece was sold or given away.

An error popular with the earlier writers on English silver was the assumption that the artistic responsibility for any piece of silver rested with the owner of the mark which was stamped upon it. It is now common knowledge that the 'maker's mark' is merely that of the goldsmith who was prepared to guarantee that the silver was of the approved standard and that he need not have had any hand in its making. Along with this error was the assumption that the original maker was responsible for all parts of the work including the engraving. It is true that the master goldsmith was expected to teach his apprentice all the skills used by the craft and that these included engraving, but the amount of knowledge imparted must have varied greatly. The wardens of the Goldsmiths were mainly out to protect the customer against dishonesty, such as the use of substandard silver and bad workmanship (e.g. the use of low quality solder). I have found in the records of the Court no instance of a goldsmith charged with bad engraving.[1] Although every apprentice may be assumed to have learnt something of engraving by the time that he had gained his freedom, this does not mean that all the work was executed by the master's regular employees or by freemen of the Company. There were freemen who made it a whole-time occupation, but there was nothing to prevent a craftsman who had learnt his skill elsewhere from decorating plate. Though the act of engraving involved the removal of an infinitesimal amount of metal, it did not affect the purity of the silver, the safeguarding of which was the main anxiety of the wardens of the Goldsmiths. The free-lance engravers were not confined to any guild and were at liberty to take any work which was offered to them. They included most of the foreigners whom we shall encounter.

The goldsmiths who were obliged by law to mark their work for the protection of the public, were not unmindful that the mark also provided an advertisement. Pieces signed by the engraver are rare probably because the goldsmith feared that he might lose his rake-off if the customer learnt to go direct to the engraver on future occasions.[2] It cannot be urged that the contribution of the engraver to the finished article was always a minor one. The round salver with a trumpet-shaped foot, so popular in the second half of the seventeenth century, is extremely dull if left unengraved. The same is true of the salvers engraved with representations of official seals in the first half of the eighteenth century.

It was rare for the customer to come into contact with the engraver.[3] The latter received his order from the goldsmith if the latter did not have an adequate craftsman in his workshop. At the end of the seventeenth century some bankers who had started as goldsmiths still continued to accept orders for plate although they had closed their workshops. It is uncertain whether Sir Richard Hoare,[4] although free of the Goldsmiths' Company, ever had a workshop but his orders for plate were passed to John Boddington and for engraving to Benjamin Rhodes with both of whom he dealt separately. After goldsmith-bankers had disappeared the free-lance engraver must have received his instructions from the goldsmith, but the latter does not seem to have had any share in the designing. This last was left to the engraver, but if he was prosperous and employed apprentices, these last might actually do the engraving. The split in responsibility within the workshop must have resulted sometimes in a talented apprentice having to carry out work in a style of which he did not approve. This must be borne in mind when the Gamble/Hogarth controversy is reached. Learning to engrave plate became a recognized means of obtaining a skill useful in other directions such as the production of prints and of book illustrations. For such work meticulous accuracy was needed and this could well be learnt in engraving plate. In times when great importance was accorded to heraldry, a blundered crest or coat-of-arms would not escape notice.

Whilst attributing great importance to the master engravers both for invention and for maintaining standards, it should be realized that even the most successful were not always original. They were always ready to copy or adapt the work of others so that it is easy to credit them with more powers of invention than is really due. A development of the nineteenth century was the provision by some architects of complete schemes of decoration for the plate which they designed.[5] This was an impingement upon the function of the master engraver but was not important since it was not widespread.

Introduction and Definitions

Notes

1. On the other hand, the minutes record on 22 January 1559 the complaint of Francis Eton who had arranged that his apprentice John Smith should be taught 'gravynge and chasynge' for the space of two years by John Leedham. After one and a quarter years had expired, he found that Leedham had been using Smith entirely on his own work and not fulfilling his obligation. The wardens ordered that Smith should remain an extra quarter with Leedham, so that the latter might teach him properly (Court Minutes 8, Pt. 1, p. 74).

2. The attitude of the goldsmiths seems ungenerous since the rare signatures are entirely unobtrusive. The public became accustomed in the eighteenth century to signed prints but the engravers were disdained. When the Royal Academy was founded in 1768, membership was confined to architects, painters and sculptors, and engravers were only made eligible as associates in 1769 but with no prospect of advancement. Full membership was only granted in 1855.

3. For the case of Thomas Bewick, see page 121.

4. Free 1672, livery 1674 and prime warden 1703.

5. Architects had been designing plate for the houses which they were building in the second half of the eighteenth century but do not seem to have bothered about engraving.

Chapter 1

1150 to 1530

W hilst the craft of engraving silver was practised in England throughout the Middle Ages, it is clear that there were periods when this form of decoration was popular and others when comparatively little use was made of it. Dr. J. M. Fritz noted the same phenomenon when dealing with the engraving of silver in Germany during the Middle Ages.[1] Only in Niedersachsen could he trace a continuous development. In England periods of activity and of inactivity were not characteristic only of the medieval period, so that it will be found that the chronological arrangement of the chapters of this book is not always the same as that used by most writers on English plate. Highly sophisticated engraving is found on the copper ciboria decorated with champlevé enamel produced in England in the second part of the twelfth century, but the only engraving on silver which has come down to us is of not nearly such high quality. The engraving on the paten (Figure 1) found with its chalice in the grave of Archbishop Hubert Walter (d. 1205) in Canterbury Cathedral, can be dated about 1160, but is much less accomplished than the scholarly inscription which adorns it. The engraving on its chalice (Figure 2) is also clumsy and compares poorly with the superb chalice and paten of about 1250 (Figures 3 and 4) found at Dolgellau. Although the evidence is scanty, it would seem that there were a number of engravers skilled in decorating chalices and patens with conventional foliage such as is found on the paten from the grave of Bishop Cantelupe (d. 1266) in Worcester Cathedral (Figure 5) and on some English chalices which have found their way to Scandinavia.[2]

Silver made in England in the first half of the fourteenth century is now extremely rare and it would seem that this was one of the periods when engraving was out of fashion.[3] This decline in popularity did not amount to a complete cessation, since it remained usual to engrave a crucifix or a cross on the foot of a chalice, whilst secular plate was sometimes engraved with an ownership mark as in the case of the *leopard's head* of the Jewel House (Figure 6) engraved on the under side of the dish of about 1330 belonging to Bermondsey Church.[4]

1, 2. CHALICE and PATEN, parcel-gilt. From the grave of
Archbishop Hubert Walter
About 1160. Chalice H. $5\frac{5}{8}$ in (14.5 cm), Paten D. $5\frac{1}{2}$ in (14 cm)
Canterbury Cathedral. See page 21

3, 4. CHALICE and PATEN, gilt. Found at Dolgellau
About 1250. Chalice H. $7\frac{1}{4}$ in (18.5 cm), Paten D. $5\frac{1}{2}$ in (14 cm)
National Museum of Wales, Cardiff. See page 21

5. PATEN, gilt
About 1250. D. 4⅝ in (12 cm)
Worcester Cathedral. See page 21

6. MARK OF THE JEWEL HOUSE on a dish
About 1330
Bermondsey Church (on loan to the Victoria and Albert Museum). See page 21

A revival of the popularity of engraving took place towards the end of the fourteenth century and long preceded the introduction into England of printing. The main advantage of printing was that it enabled designs to be copied and circulated with the greatest ease. The engravers had, however, already discovered means of duplicating designs although not with the accuracy provided by the printing press. An engraver who wished to record a design no longer had to rely upon a free-hand drawing. Thinnish paper usable for tracing, was available in Europe in the fourteenth century. Alternatively, inked pulls might be taken.[5] The advantage of tracings was that the design appeared the right way round, whereas the inked pulls were in reverse. The latter was not a serious disadvantage for any craftsman with experience in cutting seals. Inked pulls remained in use in the workshops down to the eighteenth century. They were not treasured but regarded merely as useful equipment. The use of a pull, perhaps not a very clear one, did not secure that the copyist had the skill to do full justice to the design. The dignified head of Christ engraved in about 1450 on the paten belonging to Beeston Church, Norfolk (Figure 7) is infinitely superior to the crude version on the

23

7, 8. 'The Vernicle' on patens
About 1450 (*Beeston Church, Norfolk*), and about 1480 (*Saham Tony Church, Norfolk*). *See pages 23–4*

9–11. 'The Vernicle' on patens and woodcut
About 1500 (*Hanworth Church, Norfolk*) and 1514 hallmark (*Durham Cathedral, from Heworth Church*); woodcut by Wynkyn de Worde, 1508. *See pages 23–5*

paten belonging to Saham Tony (Figure 8) in the same county. Copies taken from copies tended to become progressively worse. The introduction of printing made it possible to produce an unlimited number of copies all of equal merit. When the first English printers launched into the production of illustrated books, they did not import the more advanced woodcuts available on the Continent, but seem to have made use of what talent was available locally. It seems likely that their needs were met in part by the engravers. The arts of engraving and of cutting wood blocks are different but it is not rare for artists to be skilled in several crafts. The nature of the relationship between engraved plate and woodcuts is not always clear and it is sometimes difficult to decide which artist

24

12. PAX, parcel-gilt
About 1520. H. 5⅜ in (13·5 cm)
New College, Oxford. See page 25

was the copyist. 'The Vernicle' on the paten belonging to Hanworth Church, Norfolk (Figure 9) would appear to have been copied from a woodcut of the same subject in Wynkyn de Worde's *Dystruccyon of Jherusalem* of 1508 (Figure 11). The version on the paten of 1514 from Heworth, County Durham (Figure 10) appears to be a copy by a less skilled artist. On the other hand the engraved frame of the pax belonging to New College, Oxford (Figure 12) is much superior to the frame used by Richard Pynson in his Sarum Missal of about 1500 (Figure 13). It was a disaster both for the engravers and the printers when the religious policy of Henry VIII became more and more involved

25

13. WOODCUT from Richard Pynson's Sarum Missal of about
1500
Bodleian Library, Oxford. See page 25

and the demand for small designs of religious subjects collapsed. We may imagine that quantities of prints and inked pulls must have been scrapped during the reigns of Edward VI and Elizabeth I.

Secular woodcuts appear to have been copied more sparingly, but the Charlecote Cup[6] of 1524 (Figures 14 and 15) is engraved with beasts and monsters which probably derive from some book printed on the Continent. If this view is accepted, the interest of this piece is increased since all the other engravings which have been quoted appear to have been derived from English woodcuts.

There were always some foreign goldsmiths working in England during the Middle Ages but the latest historians[7] of the Goldsmiths' Company have pointed out that at the close of the period their number was very considerable. Thus 319 foreign goldsmiths

14, 15. THE CHARLECOTE CUP, gilt 1524 hallmark. Goldsmith's mark *comet. H. 4⅝ in (12 cm) Sir Montgomerie Fairfax-Lucy, Bart.* See page 26

were sworn to obey the rules of the Company between the years 1479 and 1510. In the four years which followed ninety-eight were added. They appear to have come mainly from the Low Countries and Germany. Not all of them can have been specialist engravers but it may be assumed that there were some. We have, therefore, to try to identify their work.

Two pieces come to mind. The first is the gold chalice and paten bearing the 1508 hallmark (Figure 16) belonging to Corpus Christi College, Oxford. The foot of the chalice is engraved with six saints (the females very fashionably dressed), each below a flamboyant traceried canopy quite unlike any used in England. The representation of the head of Christ on the paten is also suggestive of a German artist.

Next comes the case for surgical instruments, in the form of a penner, belonging to the Barber-Surgeons' Company. The back of the cover is engraved with St. George, whilst the back of the case is engraved with the martyrdom of St. Thomas of Canterbury (Figure 17). The sides of the case are engraved floral scrolls, dolphins and the sort of ornament found upon the stalls in the chapel of King's College, Cambridge. In both instances it seems best to assume that we have the more or less original designs of a German engraver working in London and not imported ones.

16. FOOT OF CHALICE, gold
1508 hallmark. Goldsmith's mark
fleur-de-lis
*Corpus Christi College, Oxford. See
page 27*

17. CASE FOR SURGICAL
INSTRUMENTS, gilt
About 1520. H. 7½ in (19 cm)
*Barber-Surgeons' Company. See
page 27*

18. 'Ecce Agnus Dei' engraved
from a 14th-century design on a
15th-century paten
*Chewton Mendip Church, Somerset.
See page 32*

19. THE STUDLEY BOWL, gilt
Late 14th century. H. 5½ in (14 cm)
Victoria and Albert Museum. See page 29

Medieval silver was not engraved only with figure subjects and conventional ornament. The popularity of inscriptions appears to have been eclipsed for the hundred years 1250 to 1350. After the Dolgellau paten (Figure 4) with its tidy Lombardic lettering, there is a gap until the earliest black-letter inscriptions of the late fourteenth century.[8] From that point inscriptions are plentiful on both religious and secular pieces down to the advent of the Renaissance. The decorative quality of the lettering is exploited in all of them but in none so successfully as on the Studley Bowl (Figure 19) which is engraved on the bowl and cover with a black-letter alphabet complete with initial cross and the usual contractions. A floral spray separates the rows of letters and the ground is lightly hatched. Late medieval plate is nearly always engraved with double-outlined lettering and with a hatched ground as on the Studley Bowl. On the other hand, the Rokewode Mazer, which is of about the same date, is unusual in having single-stroke lettering

20. THE ROKEWODE MAZER
Late 14th-century inscription
Victoria and Albert Museum. See page 29

21. MAZER with gilt rim
About 1460. H. 2 in (5 cm)
Goldsmiths' Company. See page 31

(Figure 20).[9] No capital letters appear on the Studley Bowl, but in the fifteenth century it became usual to have a capital at the beginning of the inscription, even the names of the members of the Trinity following in lower case. Only a minority of the inscriptions can be described as spontaneous, as on the Pusey Horn which seeks to bolster up a legend that William Pusey had been granted his estate by Cnut as a reward for having given a warning of a surprise attack by the Saxons. Although the inscription was

22. THE CAMPION CUP, gilt
1500 hallmark. Goldsmith's mark
covered cup. H. 3¾ in (9·5 cm)
*Victoria and Albert Museum. See
page 31*

23. SHIELD OF ARMS on the foot
of a chalice
About 1350
*Aston-by-Sutton Church, Cheshire.
See page 32*

important, since the Puseys claimed to hold their land by 'cornage' which involved the liability to produce the horn in court as evidence, the tidily engraved inscription misspells the name of the family as 'pecote'. Most of the inscriptions on secular plate are standard. Two, which are found on several mazers, are magical—the text on the label attached to Christ's cross ('Jesus Nazarenus Rex Judeorum') which was a popular charm giving protection against sudden death, and the legendary names of the Kings of Cologne (Jaspar, Melchior, Balthasar) which were credited with giving protection against epilepsy and fevers. A number of pieces carry an inscription which might be used as a grace ('Benedicam dominum in omni tempore' (Figure 21), 'Benedictus deus in donis suis', or 'Soli deo honor et gloria' (Figure 22)). More spontaneous are those enjoining social behaviour as on the Rokewode Mazer[9] and the Stradbroke Bowl.[10] Possessory inscriptions are rare, though a mazer in the British Museum carries the name of Dom Robert Pecham, a monk of Rochester Cathedral Priory, whilst another at the Victoria and Albert has the name of an otherwise unknown Robert Chalker.

By the fifteenth century inscriptions upon religious plate had likewise become standardized.[11] For chalices the favourite was ' + Calicem salutaris accipiam et nomen domini invocabo'. Those on patens were derived mainly from Holy Writ or else church services. The highly educated effusions or earlier times had vanished. Since both

31

religious and secular inscriptions had become standardized they could be reproduced with the aid of inked pulls. The clearest demonstration of this is provided by two patens of about 1520, one belonging to Cliffe-at-Hoo Church, Kent, and the other to Oscott College, Birmingham. Both are inscribed with the same black-letter inscription, '+ Benedicamus patrem et filium cum spiritu sancto', but the floral sprays which separate the words are essentially the same although obviously copied by different hands. Although this last inscription was essentially religious, it is also found used as a grace on secular plate. Black-letter inscriptions continued in use into the first quarter of the sixteenth century but latterly were competing with Roman capitals. Sometimes the two scripts were mixed.

It is strange that there are so few examples of heraldic engraving on English medieval plate. The leopard's head mark of the Jewel House has already been mentioned and some of the nobility certainly had plate engraved with their marks as can be proved by the inventory of plate in the possession of Edward II taken by Thomas of Ousefleet in 1324.[12] Although of heraldic character, these were not coats-of-arms, which were enamelled and so fall outside our subject. Engraved shields are extremely rare but two appear on the foot of the chalice belonging to Aston-by-Sutton Church, Cheshire (Figure 23). It must date around 1350 but the owners of the arms have not been identified.

Notes

1. Johann Michael Fritz, *Gestochene Bilder, Gravierungen auf deutschen Goldschmiederarbeiten der Spätgotik*, 1966.
2. C. Oman, *English Church Plate*, p. 300, plates 5 and 7.
3. This is curious because some of the best monumental brasses were being engraved about this time.
4. I discussed this dish at length in the *Burlington Magazine*, XCIV, 1952, pp. 23–6.
5. Fritz (op. cit., p. 409) records an example of an inked pull dating from the early part of the fifteenth century, in the Jagellon Library, Crakow.
6. Fully illustrated in *Apollo*, XLII, 1945, pp. 259–60.
7. T. F. Reddaway and E. M. Walker, *The Early History of the Goldsmiths' Company*, p. 171.
8. It is only possible to fill this gap with the inclusion of the Chewton Mendip paten (Figure 18) which is engraved with the lamb surrounded by 'Ecce agnus dei' in Lombardic characters. This appears to be a re-use of a fourteenth-century design on a fifteenth-century piece.
9. If modernized it reads:
    + Hold your tongue and say the best
  and let your neighbour sit in rest
  whoso listeth god to please
  let his neighbour live in ease.

10. If translated from the Latin it reads: '+ The undiluted drink renders the drinker free from care, therefore, I pray, drink as freely as you like.'
11. The subject is fully discussed in *English Church Plate*, pp. 55–8.
12. F. Palgrave, *Ancient Kalendars and Inventories of the Exchequer*, 1836, II, p. 131.

Chapter II

1531 to 1625

$\sim$ ~~ $\sim$

Since printing was introduced earlier into Germany, the engravers of that country were ahead of their English contemporaries in developing the new technique for the benefit of the goldsmiths. They did not limit themselves to printed designs for ornament but also for whole pieces. The earliest piece of English silver demonstrably inspired from a German printed design is the Masters Cup of 1535 (Figure 24) belonging to Cirencester Church, Gloucestershire, which is inspired by a design by Hans Brosamer.[1] The engraving on the Masters Cup is only minor, and the earliest example of ornament by an identified German engraver is found on the cup belonging to Gatcombe Church, Isle of Wight,[2] which has the hallmark for 1540. Round the lip is a band of foliated scrolls combined with horses' heads as invented by the Nuremberg goldsmith Lambert Hopfer. Fate has dealt especially unkindly with the plate made in the second quarter of the sixteenth century, so that it is not until after the accession of Elizabeth I that it becomes obvious how strong the influence of German printed designs had become on London goldsmiths. A group of plate given by Archbishop Parker to the colleges at Cambridge in which he was interested, shows that German influence was already being felt. The group includes an octagonal ewer and basin of 1545 with the goldsmith's mark of a *queen's head*. The sides of the ewer are alternately left plain or engraved with a moresque pattern, which also decorates the rim of the basin, which was received by Corpus Christi College. Two standing cups, one at Gonville and Caius College, with a *Moor's head* as its goldsmith's mark (Figure 25), the other at Trinity Hall, are both based on a design by Brosamer and have their bowls decorated with an elaborate moresque design. They are obviously of about the same date as the ewer and basin.[3]

The pieces already discussed can all be linked directly with the engraved designs of German goldsmiths but by the date which has now been reached printed designs were being produced also in other countries. In 1548 Thomas Geminus,[4] working in Blackfriars, was issuing sheets entitled *Morysse and Damashine Renewed*. It has not been

24. THE MASTERS CUP, gilt
1535 hallmark. Goldsmith's mark *three flowers*. H. 12⅜ in
(31·5 cm)
Cirencester Church. See page 33

25. THE PARKER CUP, gilt
About 1540. Goldsmith's mark *Moor's head*. H. 15¾ in (40
cm)
Gonville and Caius College, Cambridge. See page 33

possible as yet to connect with him the decoration of any piece of plate and his designs seem rather to be intended for use on jewellery.

Whereas in the earlier years of the reign of Henry VIII it was necessary to search carefully for examples of engraved plate, in the years covered by this chapter there is an *embarras de richesse*. It is only occasionally that we can feel certain that the actual engraver was a hundred per cent responsible for the design, and by tracing the sources which he used we get few indications of his personality. On the other hand, the English craftsmen were no mere copyists. They might have to expand a design in order to fill the space and this might require considerable ingenuity.

Economic conditions did not favour the goldsmiths and engravers during the reigns of Edward VI and Mary I, but the position was entirely altered at the accession of Elizabeth I. There was a general trend towards ornate plate and although this could be achieved by the use of several other techniques, at no subsequent period was there a larger proportion which had some engraving upon it. We shall, therefore, only be concerned with pieces on which the engraving is important. The engravers were quite

26. COMMUNION-CUP (*below*)
1564 hallmark. Goldsmith's mark *wallet hook*.
H. 6½ in (16·5 cm)
St. Michael's Church, Oxford. See page 36

27. DOUBLE BEAKER, gilt (*opposite*)
1572 hallmark. Goldsmith's mark *R F monogram*. H. 8⅞ in (22·5 cm)
Hermitage Museum, Leningrad. See page 36

35

28. COMMUNION-CUP
1568 hallmark. Mark of William Cobbold. H. 8½ in (21·5 cm)
St. Mary-at-Palace Church, Norwich. See page 36

29. COMMUNION-CUP
Dated 1576. Goldsmith's mark *IW*. H. 7½ in (19 cm)
Bodmin Church. See page 37

ready for the revival and it comes as a surprise to find how far the German sheets of designs had penetrated. This is best shown in the bands of arabesques and moresques in general use on the new communion-cups prescribed by the church authorities in order to discourage the continued use of the old medieval chalices and church services. There were two characteristic designs, one of which consisted of a narrow band of floral scroll whilst the other had panels of interlacing strap-work filled with similar scrolls. From the interlacing of the panels sometimes hang floral pendants. These not very demanding designs could be carried out in the workshops of goldsmiths who did not employ specialist engravers. There was nothing ecclesiastical about the ornament which is found also on domestic pieces. London engraved pieces in this style are illustrated by a communion-cup of 1564 (Figure 26) belonging to St. Michael's Church, Oxford, and a double beaker of 1572 (Figure 27) in the Hermitage Museum, Leningrad. Provincial goldsmiths who did not have access to specialist engravers reproduced the same designs with varying degrees of success. The decoration on the cup with the mark of William Cobbold and Norwich hallmark for 1568 (Figure 28),

30. *P over M*, attributed to
PLATE, from a set of twelve engraved with Old
Testament subjects adapted from woodcuts by
Bernard Salomon
About 1565. No contemporary hallmark and
probably executed abroad. D. 7¾ in (20 cm)
*Metropolitan Museum, New York. See pages
141–2*

31. WOODCUT by Bernard Salomon adapted by *P
over M* for the scene of 'Joseph interpreting
Pharaoh's Dream' on the plate shown as Figure
30. W. 3 in (7·5 cm)
British Museum

and on that with the initials *IW* of an unidentified Bodmin goldsmith (Figure 29), is as
good as much of what was being produced in London.

Before attempting to outline the silver engraved in the latter part of the reign of
Elizabeth I, it is necessary to discuss the very important group of pieces all decorated by
one artist and mostly signed with his initials (*P over M*). It comprises the six following
items:

1. Set of twelve plates engraved with Old Testament subjects (Figure 30). Signed *P over
   M*. No contemporary hallmarks.
2. Set of twelve plates engraved with 'The Labours of Hercules' (Figure 32). Some
   signed *P over M*. London hallmark for 1567. Goldsmith's mark *a falcon* (Thomas
   Bampton).
3. Ewer and basin engraved with the kings and queens of England, and Old Testament
   subjects (Figures 33–5). Signed *P over M*. London hallmark for 1567. Goldsmith's
   mark *L reversed*.
4. Set of twelve plates engraved with the parable of 'The Prodigal Son' (Figures 36–7
   and Frontispiece). Signed *P over M*. London hallmark for 1568 (one 1569).
   Goldsmith's mark *FR monogram*.
5. Set of six bowls, engraved with Old Testament subjects and with sea monsters
   (Figures 38–9). No signatures. London hallmark for 1573. Goldsmith's mark, *FR
   monogram*.

32. *P over M*
SET OF TWELVE PLATES, parcel-gilt, engraved with 'The Labours of Hercules' after Heinrich Aldegraver
1567 hallmark. Mark of Thomas Bampton (*falcon*). D. 7¾ in (20 cm)
Southern Comfort Corporation. See pages 45 and 142–3

33, 34 (*over page*). *P over M*
EWER and BASIN (*see over*), parcel-gilt, engraved with the sovereigns of England
and with Old Testament scenes after Bernard Salomon
Dated and hallmarked 1567. Goldsmith's mark *L reversed*. Ewer H. 13¼ in (34 cm),
Basin D. 19½ in (50 cm)
Metropolitan Museum, New York. See pages 44–5 and 143

34. *P over M*
BASIN (*see page 39*)

35.   Detail of Figure 34

36 (*opposite*), 37 (*over page*). *P over M*, attributed to
SET OF TWELVE PLATES, parcel-gilt, engraved with the parable of 'The Prodigal Son'.
1568 and 1569 hallmarks. Goldsmith's mark *FR monogram*. D. $7\frac{1}{2}$ in (19 cm)
Collection of the late Duke of Buccleuch. See page 144

36.

37.
(see
page
40)

38, 39. *P over M*,
attributed to
TWO FROM A SET OF
SIX BOWLS, silver-gilt,
engraved with Old
Testament subjects
('The Sacrifice of
Isaac' and 'The
Meeting of Isaac and
Rebecca') and with
marine subjects.
1573 hallmark.
Goldsmith's mark *FR
monogram*. D. 10 in
(25·5 cm)
*Victoria and Albert
Museum. See pages
44–5 and 144–5*

43

40, 41. *P over M*, attributed to
EWER and BASIN, parcel-gilt, engraved with Old Testament subjects after Vergil Solis and Bernard Salomon
Dated 1575. Goldsmith's mark *BI in oval*. Ewer H. 16in (41 cm), Basin D. 18 in (46 cm)
Messrs. Christie (believed to be in Germany). See pages 46 and 145–6

6. Ewer and basin engraved with Old Testament subjects and with the arms of Pallandt accolé with those of van Dorth (Figures 40–2). No signatures. Goldsmith's mark *BI in oval*. Dated 1575.

The problems raised by this group are so complicated that I have described the pieces in detail in Appendix I. Here I will only give my conclusions. With the exception of the six bowls (No. 5) the remainder of the group has been known to specialists for at least fifty years. The engraving on all of the group is manifestly by one hand, but only four carry London hallmarks. Since the engraving is unlike anything done before in England or after the years covered by the hallmarks, it is obvious that the artist was a foreigner who only visited England for a short period. Nothing much can be gleaned from the pieces decorated in England. These all have traditions going back for some centuries but never connecting with any individual who was active at the time they were made. It can scarcely be doubted that the ewer and basin (No. 3), engraved with representations of English sovereigns, was intended for presentation to Queen Elizabeth I, but evidently it never reached its destination since it is not listed in the 1574 inventory of the royal plate.[5] Although the Elizabethans were fond of decorating their plate with arms and crests, only the set of bowls (No. 5) have spaces for these and the arms are not contemporary.

It is disheartening to have to admit that the owner of the mark *P over M* remains unidentified. When attention was first focused on the group of plates engraved with 'The Labours of Hercules' (No. 2) Dr. Max Rosenheim told Sir Charles Jackson who was engaged upon his *Illustrated History of English Plate*, that this mark had been used by Peter Maes (or Maas) of Antwerp. He cannot have emphasized that this artist was reputedly only born in 1560 so that he could not have been at work in 1567. I have failed to trace in English records any artist bearing these initials, working in this country in the years 1567–74. Research into the sources of his designs has not brought to light any very valuable results. When set to decorate a ewer and basin glorifying Queen Elizabeth I and her predecessors, he had no alternative to using a set of designs produced in this country, but this source has not yet been identified.[6] For the rest he adapted the work of popular Continental artists such as Heinrich Aldegraver, Vergil Solis, Bernard Salomon and others. His preference for Old Testament subjects, in many cases complete with biblical references, makes it certain that he was a Protestant even though the text engraved round the boss on both the basins is taken from the Vulgate and not from Beza's Protestant translation. He was a decorator and not a goldsmith and all the

42. Detail of basin (Figure 41). 'The Angel sends back Hagar to Sarai'

pieces on which he worked belonged to standard patterns. After completing his work, he must have returned the pieces to the goldsmith for gilding etc. The 1575 ewer and basin (No. 6) have the backgrounds decorated with etching, a technique which was briefly popular in Germany but unknown in England.

All engravers of silver at this period made use of published designs, and in order to assess his capacity it is necessary to note how the borrowed designs fared at his hands.

43, 44. DESIGNS of Nicaise Roussel arranged by John Bar and published in 1623 *British Museum. See page 47*

The best German engravers like Heinrich Aldegraver and Vergil Solis would have had no reason to complain of his renderings of their work. It is more instructive to see how he handled the woodcuts of Bernard Salomon.[7] The latter was an indifferent artist but his little books with woodcuts of Old Testament subjects must have sold very well since his printer, Jean de Tournes, found it worth while to publish slightly varying editions with captions in Latin, French, German and Spanish. The shape and size of his cuts (6 × 8 cm) did not readily adapt to the spaces available on the plate. The engraver was not content with filling in the blanks and was ready to provide a fresh background. He never changed the poses of the figures but might make slight alterations in their dress. There can be no doubt that *P over M* was the finest engraver who had yet worked in England, but though he was capable enough as a designer and copyist we are left in

45, 46. NICAISE ROUSSEL, attributed to
LIVERY-POT, gilt.
1587 hallmark. Goldsmith's mark *TS above a two-headed eagle*. H. 15 in (38 cm)
St. Mary Woolnoth Church, London. See page 48

doubt whether he could have equalled the inventive powers of the best engravers who worked in London during the first half of the eighteenth century.

Nicaise Roussel must have arrived in England about the time or shortly after the mysterious *P over M* had left. In 1617 he was reported to have 'dwelt here 44 years'.[8] He had been born at Bruges, had a wife born in this country and eight children of whom he appears to have lost three. In the register of the Dutch Church he is listed amongst the 'Goldsmits, Diamondcuters and Jewlers within the Citye'. In 1623 John Overton published a book of his grotesques arranged by John Bar[9] and dedicated to the royal jeweller George Heriot. The dedication cannot have helped much as Heriot died in the following year but the book was twice re-issued before the end of the century. Although Roussel appears to have had a long active life we are only able to recognize a few of his

47

47. NICAISE ROUSSEL, attributed to
GOBLET, gilt
1587 hallmark. Goldsmith's mark *IN monogram*. H. 5½
in (14 cm)
Goldsmiths' Company. See page 48

48. NICAISE ROUSSEL, attributed to
TANKARD, gilt
1597 hallmark. Goldsmith's mark *IH above a bear*. H.
9⅞ in (25 cm)
Christ's College, Cambridge. See page 48

works. The most notable are a pair of livery-pots hallmarked 1587 (Figures 45–6) belonging to St. Mary Woolnoth, a pair hallmarked 1594 in the Kremlin,[10] and another pair of 1601 until recently in the possession of the Mostyn family[11] and another of 1607 at Westacre Church, Norfolk. They bear the marks of different goldsmiths, which proves that Roussel was only their decorator. The combination of grotesques, monsters and plant-forms on both pairs is quite unmistakable. The decoration on a goblet of 1587 (Figure 47) belonging to the Goldsmiths' Company, and on a tankard of 1597 (Figure 48) belonging to Christ's College, Cambridge, seems to reflect his style and some more pieces might be added more tentatively. With the exception of a magdalen cup of 1573 in the Manchester City Art Gallery, which he must have engraved soon after his arrival, all these were decorated in the years 1587 to 1607, but we know that he survived for another twenty years. Did he change his style for one which was not fancied by John Bar?

48

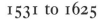

49. LID OF A MOTHER-O-PEARL BOX
About 1600. D. 3½ in (9 cm)
Victoria and Albert Museum. See page 49

The last decade of the sixteenth century was marked by new fashions for the engravers. Interlacing strap-work, panels of arabesques, roundels filled with heads were still popular but there was a very noticeable increase in the use of floral motifs (Figure 49). Botanical accuracy was seldom attempted but the artists revelled in the peculiarities of plants which were now accessible in the illustrations to Gerard's *Herbal* (1597). The flowing floral designs of the end of the reign of Elizabeth I and the beginning of that of James I are typically English and have little resemblance to similar ornament in use overseas.

Continental influence was, however, still strong and is very evident in the engraved decoration on a standing cup of 1611 in the Victoria and Albert Museum which is decorated with sports, some of which were not in use in England[12] (Figures 50-1). An almost identical cup made in the same year by the same goldsmith is at Christ's College, Cambridge, but is unengraved. This makes it worth considering whether the engraving on the first of them may have been an after-thought added some years later. If this was

50, 51. MAGDALENA or WILLEM DE PASSE, attributed to
Details of the BOWL OF A STANDING CUP
1611 hallmark, but engraving perhaps about 1615. Goldsmith's mark *TYL monogram*
Victoria and Albert Museum. See page 49

52. ENGRAVING by Magdalena de Passe, about 1619
British Museum. See page 50

the case the engraving may be credited to Willem de Passe or his sister Magdalena.[13] The latter was responsible for an engraved portrait of the Marchioness of Buckingham (Figure 52) within a passe-partout frame having a strip engraved with a bear hunt very similar to the scenes on the cup.

Although topographical prints were being produced in England in the reign of Elizabeth I there was no attempt to decorate plate in this way. The only exception is the view of a market-place on a pair of communion-flagons belonging to Cirencester Church (Figure 53). Unfortunately the plaques have no topographical value since it is impossible to recognize any of the very distinctive buildings which already adorned the town. The scene looks as if it had been copied from a woodcut such as had been used by Richard Pynson at the beginning of the century (Figure 54).

Whereas *P over M* made wide use of subjects derived from the Old and the New Testament for the decoration of the secular plate which he engraved, the decoration of religious plate was almost entirely limited to the conventional ornament which has already been described. The Recusants might have an Agnus Dei or the Crucifixion engraved on a pyx but the vast amount of Anglican plate which has survived from this period, has very little to show. Bishop Lancelot Andrewes was very prone to discourse on the parable of the Good Shepherd, which had been much used by Early Christian artists but neglected in medieval times. It is, therefore, to the influence of Andrewes that we must attribute the re-appearance of this subject. On a flagon of 1619 belonging to Severn Stoke, Worcestershire, there is a delightful representation of 'The Good Shepherd' (Figure 55) in contemporary dress. Elsewhere he is shown in conventional dress, probably adapted from the woodcuts in the Bibles of the period. 'The Three Maries', engraved upon a chalice of 1610 belonging to Beddgelert Church (Figure 56), is a less obvious choice. It is not an inspired work and one feels that the donor, Sir John Williams, might have found a better engraver, since he was the king's goldsmith. A few more subjects can be found but these will suffice.

The new families which rose to prominence under the Tudors and early Stuarts were

53. LID OF A COMMUNION-FLAGON or LIVERY POT
1577 hallmark. Goldsmith's mark *RH monogram*
Cirencester Church. See page 50

54. WOODCUT showing a town in Richard Pynson's *Cronicle of Englonde*, 1510
British Museum. See page 50

55. Detail of a COMMUNION-FLAGON engraved with 'The Good Shepherd'
1619 hallmark. Goldsmith's mark *IL above estoile*
Severn Stoke Church, Worcestershire (on loan to Victoria and Albert Museum). See page 51

56. Detail of CHALICE engraved with 'The Three Maries'
1610 hallmark. Goldsmith's mark *RS above a rose Beddgelert Church, Gwynedd (on loan to National Museum of Wales, Cardiff). See page 51*

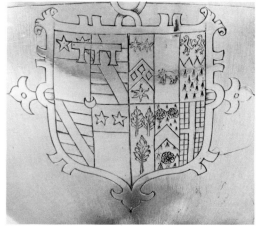

57. Detail of a COMMUNION-CUP engraved with the arms of Henry Bernay
1568 hallmark. Mark of Affabel Partridge (*bull's head*)
Reedham Church, Norfolk. See page 53

58. Detail of the REDGRAVE BACON CUP. Arms of Nicholas, third son of Sir Nicholas Bacon.
1573 hallmark. Goldsmith's mark *a bird*
British Museum. See page 53

very interested in heraldry which might be used as evidence of a more distinguished lineage than was allowed by gossip. On the other hand, they used plate as a form of currency, so that a piece might be passed on to a new owner within a matter of months. Whilst the goldsmiths produced plate with blank shields, these tended to be filled with pounced rather than the more permanent engraved coat-of-arms. For this reason we have the anomaly that during a period when heraldry was flourishing, engraved coats-of-arms are rare. Engraving was only used when the piece was being given to a church or other institution, or else specifically intended for a family heirloom. The arms on the communion-cup of 1568 (Figure 57) are typical of the ordinary work of the period. The execution was careful but the effect lifeless. Even when the customer was of importance and the intention was to create an heirloom, the result might not be much better. Sir Nicholas Bacon who had served as Lord Keeper of the Great Seal during the first twenty years of the reign of Elizabeth I, decided in 1574 to use the silver from the discarded seal of Mary I (a recognized perquisite) to make a cup for each of his three sons, for whom he had provided estates at Gorhambury, Redgrave and Stewkey. The standard of the engraving can be judged from one of those on the Redgrave cup (Figure 58) in the British Museum. No really imaginatively engraved coat-of-arms appears to have survived from the reigns of Elizabeth I and James I.

Finely lettered inscriptions are also rare. The fashion for engraving a grace round the lip of a loving-cup disappeared about the time of the accession of Elizabeth I. Most graces had been in Latin and were suggestive of popery.[14] In some areas Elizabethan communion-cups and patens have possessory inscriptions such as 'THE TOWNE OF HALESWORTH' (Suffolk) or 'ECH ENE R PAR IESE' (i.e. Itchenor parish, near Chichester). The Roman capital lettering ranges from mediocre to crude. Donative inscriptions on secular plate are only artistically important when forming part of the original design, such as that on the basin at Winchester College where it recalls re-fashioning in 1563 as well as the old Wiccamical tag 'MANERS MAKET MAN QVOTHE WYLLYAM WYKEHAM'. The inscriptions are carefully executed in Roman capitals and about the best examples of the lettering on plate at this period.[15]

Donative inscriptions of the reign of James I are generally artistically unimportant, but that on the back of the gold dish or paten belonging to the chapel of the Marquess of Exeter at Burghley House[15] is a *tour de force* of engraved cursive lettering, as well as of great literary interest. It is a pity that its minute lettering and the lightness of the engraving make it quite impossible to photograph.

Notes

1. Evidently loose sheets of Brosamer's designs must have been circulating before the publication of his *Kunst Buchlein* in 1545.
2. Illustrated in *Exhibition of Ecclesiastical Plate of Domestic Origin* at Christie's, 1955, Plate IV.

3. It would be fascinating to know who was the original owner of these pieces. Parker seems to have liked fine plate but he was only master of Corpus by the time that Henry VIII died. He became dean of Lincoln in 1552 but had to go into concealment during the reign of Mary I since he had supported the cause of Lady Jane Grey. The archbishop also presented to Corpus a pair of two-handled cups, but the decoration on them is flat-chased and not engraved.

4. He described himself as 'Lysiensis' which has been taken to mean that he came from Lys-le-Lannoy, sixteen miles north-east of Lille. He was in England in 1540 until about 1563 when it is supposed that he died. For some years he drew a pension from the Privy Purse. His best known works are anatomical illustrations and maps.

5. A. Jeffries Collins, *Jewels and Plate of Queen Elizabeth I*, 1955. The manuscript is Add. 9772 in the British Library.

6. The book of the *Genealogie of Kynges* published by Giles Godhed, 1560–2, has a series of representations of kings in which those of the Tudors are portraits, but these are not really close to those on the basin and must have been derived from some other series. Those of the earlier kings bear no relationship to those on the ewer.

7. In her valuable study on the plates in the Metropolitan Museum, Yvonne Hackenbroch (*Bulletin of the Metropolitan*, Summer 1960) tended to overstress the importance of the borrowings from Bernard Salomon—he was only one of the sources of *P over M*. The latter took great liberties in adapting the woodcuts, and his backgrounds often bear no relationship to the originals, e.g. the woodcut (Figure 31) showing 'Joseph interpreting Pharaoh's Dream' does not show the parrot-cage which is so conspicuous on the plate (Figure 30).

8. Huguenot Society, *Returns of Aliens*, X, pt. 11, 1903, p. 262.

9. Joan Evans in her article on Huguenot goldsmiths in England (*Proceedings of the Huguenot Society*, XV, 1935, p. 56) followed Guilmard (*Les Maitres Ornamentistes*, p. 42) in supposing Roussel to have been born in Lorraine because of the cross of Lorraine in the bottom left-hand corner of the prints, where it matches the *JB* in the opposite corner. Clearly it was John Bar who came from Lorraine.

10. C. Oman, *The English Silver in the Kremlin*, 1961, plate XIVa.

11. Now divided between the Manchester Art Gallery and Temple Newsam, Leeds.

12. Hunting wild boars and wild cattle.

13. A. M. Hind (*History of Engraving in England*, I, p. 19) did not know of any evidence that Magdalena visited England. She ordinarily lived with her father at Utrecht but it seems highly probable that she visited London whilst her brothers Simon and Willem were working there. Willem was in London in 1616 when he signed a portrait of Anne of Denmark but may have been there some years earlier. The claim of Willem has to be considered, since the signature of Magdalena is on the portrait and not upon the passe-partout frame.

14. English inscriptions were evidently regarded as safe, so that the two cups presented by John Blenerhasset in 1561 to the City of Norwich are inscribed 'AL MI TRVST IS IN GOD'.

15. Illustrated in *The Connoisseur*, CXLIX, 1962, p. 25.

16. In 1598 whilst Ben Jonson was in prison in Newgate awaiting trial for having killed a man in a duel, he was converted by a recusant priest. In 1609 he decided to revert to Anglicanism but found that the way back was not too easy. He decided to win acceptance by the presentation to the Earl of Salisbury of a little gold dish (diameter $6\frac{3}{4}$ in (17·2 cm)) inscribed on the under-side with a poem in memory of Lord Burghley. The complete poem appears in the folio edition of Jonson's works and is described as 'An Epigram on William Lord Burleigh Lord High Treasurer of England presented upon a plate of gold to his son, Robert Earl of Salisbury, when he was also Treasurer'. The printed version is eleven lines longer than the engraved. It may be presumed that Jonson's purse would not have allowed for a dish large enough to take all that he had penned. Jonson eventually came to the conclusion that he had not got full value for his money, for in 1618 he confided to Drummond of Hawthornden that 'Salisbury never cared for any man longer nor he could make use of him.'

Chapter III

1626 to 1699

The death of James I coincided with the close of a period in the history of English silver. The reign of James had seen a gradual deterioration of the national economy in ways which directly affected the goldsmiths and the engravers. Although Charles I was a much more enlightened patron of the arts than had been his father, his preference was more for embossed plate. Although his taste for the Dutch style of the van Vianen workshop was not as yet much imitated, the fashionable presentation pieces like salts and steeple-cups did not generally give much scope for the engravers. In the reign of Elizabeth I decorative lettering was quite common, but in that of her successor inscriptions, whether in capitals or cursive, make little pretence to be more than informative. Whilst the engravers were being squeezed out from the decoration of plate they were not having an entirely unhappy time since they had discovered fresh outlets for their skill through a closer alliance with the printers. This was not confined to illustrating books, topographical views and decorative maps, since a craze for portraiture arose similar to that which arose in the nineteenth century after the invention of photography. We are left with the curious phenomenon that during a period when there were in this country plenty of engravers, good or indifferent, English or foreign, the second quarter of the seventeenth century has to be dismissed as a dead period. If there was any important engraved silver produced, it must have perished in the Civil War.

Decorative engraving was not, of course, entirely abandoned but it was used sparingly on pieces of secondary importance, such as on beakers on which the bands of floral decoration are much inferior to those being produced in Holland. The most important development of this period was, however, the increasing attention given to heraldic engraving. There were several causes for this. Foremost was the publication in 1610 of John Guillim's *Display of Heraldry* with its systematic approach to the subject. It went through three editions before 1650 and its popularity was not affected by the republican interlude. It might be held, in fact, that the improvement in heraldic engraving dates

59. Detail of CHALICE. Arms of Poyntz
1646 hallmark. Goldsmith's mark *T B
monogram*
*North Ockendon Church, Essex (on loan to
Victoria and Albert Museum). See page 57*

60. Detail of TANKARD. Arms of Dr. Thomas Eden
1635 hallmark. Goldsmith's mark *orb and star*
Trinity Hall, Cambridge. See page 57

61. Detail of SALVER. Arms of Barrington
1660 hallmark. Goldsmith's mark *orb*
Goldsmiths' Company. See page 57

62. Detail of TANKARD. Arms of Horneby
1683 hallmark. Goldsmith's mark *WH above a crown*
Emmanuel College, Cambridge. See page 57

only from the years of the Commonwealth. The standard heraldic arrangement used in the reign of Charles I consisted merely of a square-topped shield within a laurel-wreath (Figure 59) or surmounted by a helmet with crest and flowing mantling (Figure 60). The popularity of pounced heraldry declined from the middle of the century, perhaps because there was much less plate in existence and those who were so fortunate as to have some were intent on retaining it for their own use and did not intend to pass it on within a short time. Although much of the best heraldic engraving of the second half of the seventeenth century records donorship, a greater proportion was decorated for customers who intended to retain it for their own use. Another change was the gradual adoption of the practice of hatching according to an agreed code in order to indicate the heraldic colours. It had begun to be used abroad about 1600 but was only popularized about thirty years later by the Jesuit Petra Sancta and the Franco-Scot Wilson de la Colombière. This device greatly aids the identification of arms but was very slow in winning acceptance in England.[1] Although pioneers were already using this device in the reign of Charles I many of the best engravers were ignoring it in the early eighteenth century. The commonest heraldic arrangement used by the engravers of the latter part of the century, showed a square shield with a straight or three-pointed top surrounded by ostrich-plumes tied together. Some engravers, however, improved on this design which was used much too often, by adding a floral surround (Figure 61). Later, the plumes might be replaced by crossed palm-branches or by crossed branches with flowers (Figure 62).

All the armorials which have been illustrated have been taken from pieces of secondary importance, but after the Restoration the manufacture of really expensive plate was resumed. Although much of it was decorated in ways that did not require the co-operation of an engraver, opportunities for superior artists were becoming more plentiful. The ewer and basin of 1677 presented by Samuel Pepys to the Clothworkers' Company, with its spirited rendering of the arms of the Company (Figure 63) and imaginative panel on the rim for the inscription (Figure 64), illustrate the increased appreciation of the art of engraving which was able to convert a merely massive piece of plate into a masterpiece.

It is disappointing that it is even more difficult to name the engravers of this period than to do so for the goldsmiths whose work they decorated. It is disappointing that the information to be gleaned regarding the goldsmiths' largest customer is so ambiguous. Charles II, of course, took no interest in the royal plate, but the royal patronage was of great importance since at the Restoration it fell to the Lord Chamberlain (the Earl of Pembroke) to replace what had been lost under the Commonwealth. Sir Gilbert Talbot was appointed Master of the Jewel House in July 1660, and shortly afterwards secured the appointment of Robert Viner as Royal Goldsmith. These two worked together for the rest of the reign, Viner dying in 1688 and Talbot retiring in 1690. Viner was not a practising goldsmith but distributed the orders amongst the favoured craftsmen whose

63, 64. Details of the PEPYS BASIN
1677 hallmark. Goldsmith's mark *IS interlaced*
Clothworkers' Company. See page 57

marks appear upon the plate. It was the ordinary practice for the goldsmith to select the engraver but in this case the engravers appear to have been appointed, as follows, by the warrant of the Lord Chamberlain:[2]

4 May 1661 'Edward Smyth sworne in the place of Engraver in ordinary to his Ma[tie]'
8 March 1669 'William Shirwin Engraver in ordinary, assistant to the Chief Engraver'

Engraver Extraordinary

19 August 1664 John Destach
23 February 1668 Richard Hutton

I have failed to discover anything further about these individuals but since the Lord Chamberlain had appointed on 12 October 1660 an 'Engraver in Copper', it seems clear that they cannot have formed part of the printing establishment.

On the death of Sir Robert Viner in 1688, he was succeeded as Royal Goldsmith by a nephew of the same name who had been made free of the Goldsmiths' Company in 1678

65. Detail of CADDINET. Arms of Charles II updated for William and Mary
1683 hallmark. Goldsmith's mark *WE*
Jewel House, H.M. Tower of London, by gracious permission of H.M. the Queen. See page 61

and was a practical goldsmith. He died in 1690 but in the few months of his tenure of the office, a lot of engraving had to be done for the Jewel House. It was customary to engrave the royal plate with the arms and initials of the new sovereign whenever a change occured. This was doubly necessary at the time of the Glorious Revolution since it would have been embarrassing for William III to be served on plate bearing the arms of his father-in-law whom he had just deposed. This is illustrated by the engraving on two caddinets[3] which have recently been put on exhibition with the Regalia in the Tower, after having been in private possession since 1808. The earlier caddinet bears the hallmark for 1683 and goldsmith's mark *WE between two mullets*. The rendering of the arms is spirited and they have been brought up to date by the insertion of William's inescutcheon of Nassau. The clumsy monogram used by William and Mary

66. 'MASTER OF GEORGE VERTUE', Attributed to
Detail of CADDINET. Arms of William and Mary 1688–9
1688 hallmark. Mark of Anthony Nelme
Jewel House, H.M. Tower of London, by gracious permission of H.M. the Queen. See page 61

67. 'Master of George Vertue', attributed to
Detail of TANKARD. Arms of Martha Lydall
1683 hallmark. Goldsmith's mark *EG below quatrefoil*
Private collection. See page 62

replaced the original initial of Charles II (Figure 65). The second caddinet bears the goldsmith's mark of Anthony Nelme and hallmark for 1688. The arms reflect a temporary emergency resulting from the fact that the link between the kingdoms of England and Scotland was a personal one and the Scots were in no great hurry to transfer their allegiance from James VII. The Scottish Parliament finally acknowledged William and Mary on 11 April 1689, which was the day fixed for the coronation in London. The news cannot have arrived in London until some days later so that the arms on the caddinet make no allusion to Scotland, the arms of Ireland appearing in both the second and third quarters (Figure 66).

It is obvious that the engraver of the 1688 caddinet was not the same individual who had decorated the one of 1683, and it is possible to recognize his mannerisms in the engraving on a number of other pieces made at the end of the seventeenth century. His armorial supporters are shown with their feet resting safely upon a bracket whereas most engravers showed them supported on nothing more substantial than the scroll which bore the motto. His lions are recognizable whether seen in profile or full face. Two tankards show typical examples of his work. One which bears the 1683 hallmark,

68. 'MASTER OF GEORGE VERTUE', attributed to
detail of TANKARD. Arms of William and Mary
1692 hallmark. Mark of George Garthorne
Bank of England. See page 62

with goldsmith's mark *EG below a quatre foil*, shows the arms of Martha Collins widow
of Robert Lydall of Didcot, Berkshire (Figure 67). The widow's arms are on a lozenge
surrounded by a cartouche round which is draped the widow's rosary (*cordelliera*), a
feature most unusual in English heraldry, being tainted with popery.[4] The pair of
snarling lions supporting shields probably survive from some earlier use of the design
for some more exalted person. They reappear, more appropriately, on a tankard made
by George Garthorne in 1692 for Queen Mary II, for presentation to a Dutch captain
who had carried her husband safely to Holland after a stormy voyage (Figure 68). Less
elaborate armorials showing this artist's mannerisms are not uncommon.[5]

A quite different type of composition which seems to reflect the same artist's
handiwork, appears on the superb toilet-set made by Pierre Harache in 1695 which is
still mainly the property of the Marquess of Exeter, though some pieces were sold at the

69. 'MASTER OF GEORGE VERTUE', attributed to
LID OF COMB-BOX
1695 hallmark. Mark of Pierre Harache
Messrs. Christie. See page 63

end of last century. The design on the lid of the comb-box (Figure 69) reappears, slightly altered on an oval salver in the Werner Collection, at Luton Hoo. At the bottom are seen two lions reposing on a platform, separated by two cornucopiae and a cipher below the coronet of a marchioness. Two trumpeting cupids would not appear to have disturbed the quiescent lions. Around the sides of the casket are engraved amorini, quivers, cornucopiae etc. Attempts[6] have been made to attribute the engraving on this toilet-set to Simon Gribelin whose work will be discussed in the next chapter, but it seems wiser to credit it to a shadowy character mentioned by Horace Walpole in his bibliographical note on George Vertue who was born in 1684 and at 'about the age of thirteen was placed with a master who engraved arms on plate and had the chief business in London; but who being extravagant, broke, and returned to his own country, France, after Vertue had served him between three and four years. As the man was unfortunate, though by his own fault, the good nature of the scholar has concealed his name.'[7] This decision, which Walpole regarded as over-scrupulous, has left me with no alternative but to refer to him as the 'Master of George Vertue' until his true name is

63

70. *HR conjoined*
TABLE-TOP engraved with the arms of William III
About 1700. Mark of Andrew Moore. W. 48 in (122 cm)
Windsor Castle, by gracious permission of H.M. the Queen. See page 64

discovered. It is probable that he was not a Huguenot since he voluntarily returned to France, and there were a number of other countries willing to accept distressed French Protestants.

The 'Master of George Vertue' is not the only first-class engraver who was active in London but whose identity has not been established. The most important item in the collection of silver furniture at Windsor Castle is a table which is traditionally supposed to have been presented by the merchants of the City of London to William III. Its exact date cannot be fixed since it bears no hallmark but only the goldsmith's mark used by Andrew Moore and registered in April 1697. The top (Figure 70) has in the centre an oval containing the royal arms and supporters surrounded by military trophies, whilst the four corners have the emblems of England, Scotland, Ireland and France on cartouches surrounded by cherubs amidst scroll-work. On the trail of one of the two cannons at the bottom of the central panel is the signature *HR* (conjoined) *Scup* (Sculpsit).[8] Who was *HR*? Although his style is obviously indebted to some of the contemporary Continental engraved ornament, it is quite distinct from that of either the 'Master of George Vertue' or that of Simon Gribelin which will be studied in the next chapter.

64

71. Detail of PATEN engraved with 'The Virgin and Child' after Dürer
1671 hallmark. Mark of Ralph Leake
Southwell Cathedral. See page 65

The London engravers of plate in the late seventeenth century were seldom able to escape from heraldic designs. Although the church plate was frequently engraved with the sacred monogram, figure subjects are rare. Recusant chalices and pyxes might have the Crucifixion or the Agnus Dei. An interesting exception on Anglican plate is a Virgin and Child on a paten of 1671 at Southwell Cathedral (Figure 71), which is a copy in reverse of a Dürer print dated 1512.

In Holland there is a long tradition of engraving genre subjects on silver but these rarely appear on English plate. The most notable examples of this period are connected with the two most sensational events of the early years of the reign of Charles II. On 17 October 1666, the Earl of Manchester, Lord Chamberlain, signed a warrant for the provision of 800 ounces of white plate as a gift from the king to Sir Edmund Berry Godfrey in recognition of his assiduity in attending to his duties as a City magistrate during the Plague of 1665 and the Fire of 1666.[9] Some years later Godfrey seems to have decided to have the gift (probably a wine-cooler) converted into gifts for his friends. There survive a tankard of 1673, and five more and a flagon of 1675. On the front of each are engraved the royal arms above those of Godfrey, on one side a representation of the plague victims being carried away for burial (Figure 72) and on the other the burning of the City (Figure 73). The two scenes are quite unworthy of the important occasions which they commemorate and would not have satisfied Sir Robert

72, 73. Details on a Berry Godfrey TANKARD. Scenes representing the Plague and the Great Fire
1675 hallmark. Goldsmith's mark *IN above a bird*
The Earl of Lonsdale. See page 65

74. TOBACCO-BOX engraved with a view of Norwich
About 1696. Goldsmith's mark *IH between two stars*. W. 3¾ in (9·5 cm)
Victoria and Albert Museum. See page 66

Viner or the officials of the Jewel House who handled the order for the original gift. Whilst the engraving on the Godfrey plate is merely dull, there is a certain naive charm about the decoration of a tobacco-box on the lid of which is a cipher surrounded by a scene depicting a wagon drawn by five horses and in the background a town which can be recognized as Norwich (Figure 74). It must date before 1696 since the goldsmith's mark, *IH between two stars*, is of the type in use before the introduction of the Britannia Standard.

There is no sign of any specially competent engraver being employed by the provincial goldsmiths during the reign of Charles I but some outstanding artists were available during the second half of the century. John Plummer of York was the most important

75. PEG-TANKARD engraved with a mock botanical design
1657 York hallmark. Mark of John Plummer. H. 7¼ in (18·5 cm)
Victoria and Albert Museum. See page 67

76. PEG-TANKARD engraved with a mock botanical
design
1663 York hallmark. Mark of John Plummer. H. 7½ in
(19 cm)
Lord Gisborough. See page 67

provincial goldsmith of this period and had a taste for original engraving. There survive
six peg-tankards bearing the York hallmarks respectively for 1656 (two), 1657, 1659,
1663 and 1669. They are decorated with floral designs of a mock botanical character.
For instance, by 1656[10] it was common knowledge that tulips grew from bulbs (Figure
75), whilst the 1663 tankard is decorated in a manner which seems to anticipate the
'Garden of Live Flowers' in *Alice in Wonderland* (Figure 76). Since these tankards are all
of the Scandinavian type mounted on three feet, it would be tempting to suggest that
the engraver came from across the North Sea. The accompanying heraldic engraving is,
however, typically English so that we can only conclude that Plummer had discovered a
really original artist. Although sometimes borrowing the ideas of Nicaise Roussel, he
was able to use them much more effectively than had his master.

A few years later Plummer discovered another engraver who could handle
topographical subjects as well as heraldry. Ripon Cathedral possesses a set of
communion-plate which was given at Easter 1676 by two benefactors, Jonathan
Jennings, Esq., and Prebendary Henry Greswold. The chalices are engraved with the
arms and crest of Jennings whilst the remaining pieces have the Agnus Dei which was
used as its crest by the minster. All of the pieces are engraved with a representation of
the cathedral showing it complete with the spire on the central tower (Figure 77), which
had been lost in a storm in 1660, and the two others removed in 1664 lest they should

77. COVERED PATEN engraved
with a view of Ripon Cathedral
about 1660
1675 York hallmark. Mark of John
Plummer. H. 9¼ in (23·5 cm)
Ripon Cathedral. See page 67

78. PEG-TANKARD engraved with
a view of Pontefract Castle about
1650
1680 York hallmark. Mark of John
Plummer. H. 7¼ in (18·5 cm)
Messrs. Christie. See page 69

79. LEMUEL KING OF OXFORD
Details of BASIN with arms of the College
1685 hallmark. Goldsmith's mark *IR above crown*
St. John's College, Oxford. See page 70

suffer the same fate. It is curious that this retrospective feature also appears on another piece bearing the mark of John Plummer and the York hallmark for 1680. It is a tankard engraved with a view of Pontefract Castle (Figure 78) which is shown as it had been before the Civil War when it had been slighted by the Parliamentarians after it had been desperately defended by the Royalists.

The heraldic engraving on plate made at the other provincial centres was often as good as what was being produced at the same time in London. A question mark must remain regarding the engraving on plate given to the universities of Oxford and Cambridge.

80, 81. LEMUEL KING OF OXFORD
Details of a PORRINGER. Arms of Sir John Pakington, Bart. and of the College
1689 hallmark. Goldsmith's mark *II above fleur-de-lis*
St. John's College, Oxford. See page 70

Gifts appear generally to have been sent down to the university already engraved in London. Occasionally, however, a bursar might receive a gift direct from the donor and might entrust the engraving to a local artist. It is sad that so little has come to light with regard to Lemuel King of Oxford. He was first noticed by E. Alfred Jones[11] who states that he had been apprenticed to Daniel Porter, goldsmith, of Oxford, who was probably also an engraver of silver. Both King and Porter are mentioned by Anthony Wood, mainly in connection with drinking parties in taverns, but he is described as living in the parish of All Saints.[12] In 1685 John Kent presented a ewer and basin (Figure 79)[13] to St. John Baptist College, Oxford. The arms are surmounted by two cherubs and framed by swags of fruit. Between the arms and the latter is engraved *L. King Sculpsit*. Four years later the college received a two-handled cup from Sir John Pakington, Bart., whose arms appear on one side with those of the college on the other (Figures 80–1).[14] The artist's signature appears beneath the arms of the donor. Whilst King's heraldry is as good as that of any London engraver the composition of the college arms is as charming as anything produced by the French engravers at work in the capital.

By the close of the Caroline period the engravers had recovered most of the ground lost during the reign of Charles I and in 1700 the outlook appeared most promising. In one field, however, not much progress had been made. None of the engravers appear to have interested themselves in calligraphy. The lettering, whether in capitals or cursive, is invariably undistinguished.[15]

Notes

1. It is well to examine with care pieces on which heraldic hatching appears at an unusually early date, since in the past some collectors have had the original arms taken out and replaced by their own leaving, however, the original ornamental surround. When this has been done there are usually signs of tampering on the back. There was nothing fraudulent about this such as is the case when a plain piece is engraved with the arms of a long-deceased notability to whom it never belonged.

2. Public Records Office, LC3/26, pp. 49, 166. John Destach was probably a Frenchman and related to Michael Destaches who was granted denization about this time. We hear of no further appointments to these posts. Were the engravers as long-lived as Talbot and Viner, or did the Lord Chamberlain come to leave it to the Royal Goldsmith to pick his engravers?

3. The caddinet was a piece of plate introduced by Charles II for use by members of the royal family when dining in state. It had an oblong tray engraved with the royal arms and having at one end a box with compartments for cutlery and salt. The tray, which was engraved with the arms, was intended to carry a napkin. For a full discussion see *Burlington Magazine*, C, 1960, pp. 431–5.

4. The same feature appears on a box made before 1697 for the widowed Lady Capell of Tewkesbury (J. D. Davis, *English Silver at Williamsburg*, 1976, no. 211).

5. e.g. on a pair of two-handled cups made in 1694 for Hans William Bentinck, first Earl of Portland (C. Oman, *Catalogue of Plate belonging to the Bank of England*, 1967, no. 15 plate V).

6. Michael Clayton, *Dictionary*, p. 35; John Hayward, *Huguenot Silver*, pl. 88.

7. *Anecdotes*, p. 469.

8. Although the inscription is quite tidily engraved it has been misread in both the standard accounts. Sir Guy Laking (*Furniture of Windsor Castle*, 1905, p. 29) gives 'R H SCAP', whilst John Hayward (*Huguenot Silver*, p. 69) gives 'RHS'.

9. P.R.O., LC/5-107, p. 114.

10 A duplicate of Figure 75, but with the arms of Malbrick and hallmark for 1656, was in the hands of Messrs. Spink in 1976.

11. *The Times*, 18 April 1942.

12. *Life and Times of Anthony Wood*, III, p. 260.

13. Goldsmith's mark *IR between four pellets*.

14. Goldsmith's mark *I.I.*

15. The only form of calligraphy which became increasingly popular was the use of ciphers of initials. These tend to be so intricate as to be virtually impossible to identify by anyone who does not already know the answer.

Chapter IV

1700 to 1765

The artists who brought about a change of fashion around the year 1700 had all been at work before that date.[1] Hitherto we have been dealing with long periods during which only occasionally has it been possible to name an artist. During the first half of the eighteenth century the names of a number of engravers are known and it is possible to trace links between many of them. The subject of artistic genealogies will be treated more fully in Appendix II. The master to whom an apprentice was bound to learn his craft may be presumed to have been an engraver. This becomes still more certain when it is found that the master or his master had been apprenticed to a known engraver. Whilst the master was under obligation to impart his technical skill to his apprentice, the latter did not necessarily like his master's style and when he had served his time developed his own. The field for research is not confined to the records of the Goldsmiths' Company, since it was only necessary for anyone wishing to work within the City to be free of one of the livery companies. Those wishing to specialize in the engraving of plate often joined the Goldsmiths' Company. On the other hand Simon Gribelin (to whom we shall return) joined the Clockmakers as was natural for a member of a family with a long tradition of watch-making in France. It is difficult to explain why a series of engravers of plate sought the freedom of the Merchant Taylors. Probably other companies were equally accommodating. A further complication is added by the fact that at the beginning of the period which has been reached, there was a large number of Huguenot craftsmen at work in London who had gained a reputation for circumventing regulations.

The return to France of the 'Master of George Vertue' in about 1700 left Simon Gribelin as the leading engraver of silver in London. He had been born in 1661 at Blois, a town noted both for Protestantism and for watch-making. An earlier Simon Gribelin had been making watches as far back as 1588 and examples of the work of his son Abraham are in the British Museum and the Victoria and Albert Museum. Walpole tells us that the young Simon Gribelin 'came to England in about 1680; but it was about

82. SIMON GRIBELIN
Title-page of *A Book of Ornaments*, 1697
British Museum. See page 73

twenty years before he was noticed'.[2] The slowness of his rise to fame may be accounted for by his concentrating at first on the decoration of watch-cases, watch-cocks and small sweetmeat and snuff-boxes. In 1697 he issued a little book of engravings entitled *A Book of Ornaments usefull to jewellers, watch-makers & all other artists* and followed this in 1700 by *A Book of Ornaments usefull to all Artists*. Both were mainly concerned with the decoration of watches and fancy goods but it will be noticed that the border of the title-page of the 1697 booklet was suitable for the border of a silver table-top (Figure 82). His style is admirably illustrated in the title-page of the 1700 booklet (Figure 83). Walpole's criticism was that 'his works have no more merit than finicalness, and that not in perfection.' Though it is easy to see what displeased Walpole, it is possible after an interval of two hundred years to view his work with greater appreciation. This is

73

83. SIMON GRIBELIN
Title-page of *A Book of Ornaments*, 1700
British Museum. See page 73

made easier because he sometimes signed his work but also because there is in the Print Room of the British Library an album with a manuscript title-page 'Livre d'Estampes de Sim. Gribelin fait Relié à Londre 1722'.[3] It is filled with a collection of prints, proofs and counter-proofs selected by the artist from his own work. Besides pages from his two booklets of engraved ornament there are a series of engravings issued in 1707, of the Raphael Cartoons, of old master paintings in the Royal Collection issued in 1712, the ceiling of the Banqueting House in Whitehall issued in 1722, besides illustrations for anatomical, botanical, and topographical books. Although information about Simon Gribelin's activities is more than usually plentiful, caution must be exercised in attributing work to him. Whereas engravers tended to postpone publishing their designs until they were on the verge of retirement, he survived the appearance of his first booklet by thirty-eight years and according to Walpole was active until the last. There was plenty of time, therefore, for hints from his work to creep into the engravings of other artists. Added to this there is the problem presented by Simon's son Samuel who will be mentioned shortly.

What is probably the earliest surviving piece decorated by Simon Gribelin, is a small oval comfit-box at the Victoria and Albert Museum.[4] Unfortunately it has been much rubbed in the course of time so that a pull contained in the Gribelin album gives a better impression of it (Figure 84). In the centre is a double cipher surmounted by a baron's coronet and surrounded by amorous scenes with appropriate inscriptions.[5] The

84. SIMON GRIBELIN
Pull from a comfit-box (the box, which is much rubbed, is in the
Victoria and Albert Museum)
About 1690
British Museum. See page 73

signature *Sim Grib* appears in the hatched ground on either side of the bottom inscription. There is neither goldsmith's mark nor hallmark but it leaves the impression that it was decorated before the artist's main interest had passed from watches to plate. This must have taken place by 1690 by which time he was making a speciality in the decoration of salvers. These had become popular in the second half of the seventeenth century and consisted of a round dish mounted on a trumpet-shaped foot which sometimes unscrews. The Caroline engravers rarely exploited to the full the artistic possibilities of the round top and contented themselves with a simple rendering of the coat-of-arms. Gribelin's elaborate all-over decorations signified that salvers had come to be regarded as things of beauty in their own right and were no longer to be regarded as mere stands for porringers 'in giving Beer, or other liquid thing to save the

75

85. SIMON GRIBELIN
EXCHEQUER SEAL SALVER of the Earl of Halifax
About 1695. Mark of Benjamin Bathurst (?) D. 13½ in (34·5 cm)
Burrell Collection, Glasgow Art Gallery and Museum. See page 76

Carpit or Cloathes from drops'.[6] Gribelin's compositions were usually made to fit into a roundel, so that it is not always possible to decide from the pulls in his album whether they were taken from a salver or a large dish. In the album is a pull showing a roundel enclosing the head of Frederick, Duke of Schomberg, who was killed at the Battle of the Boyne in July 1690, but since it is dated, in reverse, 1689 it must have been executed whilst he was still alive. The album contains pulls from a number of other salvers or dishes which have also perished, but since they are purely armorial and uninscribed it is not possible to date them exactly.[7] This is fortunately not the case of the salvers made out of the discarded official seals of the great officers of state.[8] Hitherto these seals (with much additional silver) had usually been converted into cups, and the idea of turning them into salvers does not seem to date further back than the days of Gribelin. They were made for display and remain in perfect condition.

When Mary II died on 27 December 1694, Charles Montagu, Earl of Halifax, had been Chancellor of the Exchequer for nearly nine months. The salver which he

86. Simon Gribelin
Proof, first state, of the engraving on the Halifax Exchequer Seal Salver in the
Burrell Collection
British Museum. See page 77

commissioned is now in the Burrell Collection, Glasgow (Figure 85). It will be seen that
the ground is occupied by rich mantling against which is depicted representations of the
obverse and the reverse of the Exchequer Seal of William and Mary above those of the
Chancellor. The hallmarking of these salvers presented a problem. If they were
stamped after they had been finished, the dents would show through the engraving on
the front. If, on the other hand, they were marked first, the goldsmith would have to
flatten the dents out before handing the piece over to the engraver. The marks on the
seal salvers are nearly always indistinct. The date-letter on the present piece is illegible
but the goldsmith's mark appears to be the cipher of *BB* attributed by Jackson to
Benjamin Bathurst. In the Gribelin album is a proof taken from the salver in which the
obverse of the seal is shown askew (Figure 86). Seals of this type usually had lugs which
enabled the two halves to be applied accurately but Gribelin appears to have ignored this
aid. In the finished version the two halves are both shown upright.[9] Gribelin's work
seems to have given such satisfaction that he was awarded the engraving of the next two

77

87. SIMON GRIBELIN
Proof from the first Exchequer Seal salver of Henry Boyle
About 1702
British Museum. See page 78

88. SIMON GRIBELIN
Proof from the second Exchequer Seal salver of Henry Boyle
About 1708
British Museum. See page 78

Exchequer Seal salvers. Henry Boyle, third son of Lord Clifford of Lanesborough, held the office of Chancellor of the Exchequer from 1701 until 1708, so that he received not only the seal rendered obsolete by the death of William III but also that discarded after the union with Scotland. Both salvers are now in the possession of the Chatsworth Trustees. Only the first bears a signature *SG*, but pulls from both are in the Gribelin album (Figures 87 and 88).

The extent of Gribelin's success can be gauged by listing the goldsmiths whose marks are stamped upon the pieces he engraved: Benjamin Bathurst, Pierre Harache, Isaac Liger, Benjamin Pyne and Samuel Wastell; and the album contains pulls of pieces engraved by him for members of the aristocracy such as John Cartaret (later Lord Granville), George Hamilton, Earl of Orkney, and most frequently George Booth, second Earl of Warrington. A number of versions of the earl's arms appear in the album but not actually the design for the tea-caddy (Figure 89) with the mark of Isaac Liger and hallmark for 1706, which must clearly have been engraved by Gribelin who in the same year and for the same goldsmith engraved an altar-dish for the earl's private chapel at Dunham Massey Hall, Cheshire (Figure 90). It is engraved with 'The Deposition' after Annibale Carracci and is signed *Ann. Car. jnv. S. G. sculp.*

Gribelin enjoyed a particularly long working life — Walpole tells that he was active until

89. SIMON GRIBELIN, attributed to
TEA-CADDY, gilt, with arms of the Earl of
Warrington
1706 hallmark. Mark of Isaac Liger. H. 4¼ in
(11·5 cm)
Victoria and Albert Museum. See page 78

90. SIMON GRIBELIN
Detail of gilt ALTAR-DISH with engraving of 'The Deposition' after Annibale
Carracci
1706 hallmark. Mark of Isaac Liger
National Trust (Dunham Massey Hall). See page 78

three days before his death in 1733 at the age of seventy-two. We have no documentary evidence with regard to his work in his last eleven years since the album ends in 1722 and it does not include all his earlier work. There is always a risk in attributing work to an artist who has published his designs and although Gribelin was almost the only first-class engraver at work at the beginning of the century, this was no longer the case twenty years later. Nonetheless, there are a number of items which can be attributed to him with tolerable certainty. First of all come a set of four gilt hexagonal waiters (Figure 91) with the goldsmith's mark of Benjamin Pyne and hallmark for 1698, engraved with the arms of Sir William Courtenay of Powderham Castle, Devon.[10] The *amorini* supporting a wreath above the coat-of-arms are strikingly similar to those on the title-page of his booklet of 1700 (Figure 83). No hesitation is needed before attributing to Gribelin the engraving on a large basin (Figure 92) presented together with a ewer, to

79

91. SIMON GRIBELIN,
attributed to
WAITER, gilt, engraved with the
arms of Sir William Courtenay
1698 hallmark. Mark of
Benjamin Pyne. W. 9½ in (24
cm)
*Victoria and Albert Museum. See
page 79*

92. SIMON GRIBELIN,
attributed to
BASIN, gilt, engraved with the
arms of the College and those of
Thomas Wentworth
1717 hallmark. Mark of Samuel
Wastell. D. 19½ in (49.5 cm)
*St. John's College, Cambridge.
See page 79*

93. SIMON GRIBELIN or else
the 'MASTER OF GEORGE
VERTUE' (?)
Detail of gilt BASIN engraved
with arms of Sir Benjamin
Bathurst
1700 hallmark. Mark of
Pierre Harache
Private collection. See page 81

St. John's College, Cambridge, by Thomas Wentworth of Wentworth Woodhouse, Yorkshire, in 1717. It bears the mark of Samuel Wastell. In this case the engraver based the design on that of the seal salver which he had decorated for the Earl of Halifax twenty years earlier and of which he had preserved the pulls which are in the album (Figure 86). It will be noticed that the mantling has been reproduced exactly.

A basin bearing the goldsmith's mark of Pierre Harache and the hallmark for 1700 would seem to be an early work of Gribelin although an attribution to the 'Master of George Vertue' is not unthinkable. It is a superb composition (Figure 93) showing in the centre the arms of Sir Benjamin Bathurst impaling those of his wife Frances, daughter of Sir Allen Apsley, surrounded by *amorini* and all sorts of symbols of eternal love.[11]

When the time came for apprenticing his son Samuel, Simon did not choose to enter him for a freedom by patrimony with the Clockmakers' Company but bound him to a freeman of the Goldsmiths'. He was bound first on 24 April 1710 to Philip Rollos II, but was turned over ten days later to Lewis Mettayer. Both of his masters were plate-workers, and it seems likely that the arrangement was merely a matter of convenience and that Samuel passed all his time in his father's workshop. He never took up the freedom of the Goldsmiths' Company. Walpole tells us that he 'graved in his father's manner'. It seems fair to attribute to him the engraving on two more seal salvers bearing

94. SAMUEL GRIBELIN, attributed to
Detail of gilt SEAL SALVER of the Court of Common Pleas.
Arms of Sir Robert Eyre
1728 hallmark. Mark of Edward Vincent
Messrs. Sotheby. See page 82

95. SAMUEL GRIBELIN, attributed to
Detail of gilt SEAL SALVER of the Principality of Wales. Arms
of Sir Robert Eyre
1728 hallmark. Mark of Edward Vincent
Messrs. Sotheby. See page 82

the mark of Edward Vincent and the hallmark for 1728. Both were made for Sir Robert
Eyre out of seals made obsolete by the death of George I. One was made from the seal of
the Chief Justice of the Court of Common Pleas (Figure 94) and the other for the
Principality of Wales (Figure 95). The *amorini* playing amidst foliage are very
reminiscent of the work of Simon Gribelin but the general effect lacks his vigour. This
could, of course, be due to the fact that he was already aged sixty-seven and that his
powers were declining, but it seems more probable that they were engraved by his son.
Samuel was still in London although in the following year he accompanied the Earl of
Kinnoul, who had been appointed ambassador, to Turkey.[12]

Benjamin Rhodes (or Roads) of Houghton, Nottinghamshire, was bound apprentice in
1670 to David Venables, goldsmith, and obtained his freedom in 1678, Whereas we
have no means of assessing the artistic capacity of Venables, we are able to gauge that of
Rhodes because there has survived his account-book for the plate which he engraved
for Sir Richard Hoare between 1 January 1694 and 6 January 1698. This is a little
tattered volume (7 × 6 inches) containing eighty-seven pages and contained within a
dirty vellum cover. It is one of the treasures of Hoare's Bank, by the courtesy of whose
directors I have been allowed to study it and illustrate some of its pages. The historian
of the bank was of the opinion that Richard Hoare was originally a practical goldsmith,

but that during the years under review he had become merely a retailer of plate which was made to order by several chosen goldsmiths.[13] The keeping of a shop allowed him to earn a commission whenever one of his customers decided to turn some of his capital into plate. It might have been expected that Hoare would have left it to the goldsmith to pick the engraver but he preferred to deal directly with Rhodes. This ensured his receiving his commission when a customer had occasion to wish for an alteration.[14]

On the left side of each page Rhodes drew a rough sketch of the arms to be engraved (Figure 96). He did not always bother to draw them out completely but simplified them according to a code of his own. Alternatively, he might take a counter-proof after the engraving had been completed.[15] A rendering of the arms of Charles Beauclerc, Duke of St. Albans and son of Nell Gwynne, gives a sample of his more ambitious work (Figure 97). It appeared on a large gilt salver. Although Hoare numbered as customers in these years a large number of the nobility,[16] as well as some of the new commercial aristocracy, Rhodes does not seem to have been called upon to engrave any piece of

96. Page from the ACCOUNT-BOOK of Benjamin Rhodes for engraving executed for Sir Richard Hoare. The entry relating to the Clarke Porringer given to Magdalen College is third from the top
Hoare's Bank. See page 83

97. Counter-proof of the arms of the Duke of St. Albans in the account-book of Benjamin Rhodes
Hoare's Bank. See page 83

98. BENJAMIN RHODES
THE CLARKE PORRINGER showing the engraving charged for in the account-book (Figure 96)
1685 hallmark. Goldsmith's mark *R A*
Magdalen College, Oxford. See page 84

major importance. The few examples of his work which have been identified with
certainty by means of the account-book, are only secondary, such as the arms of Henry
Boyle (later Lord Carleton) and those of the college, which appear on the cup and cover
of 1697 presented to Trinity College, Cambridge, and for which 15s. 6d. was charged
for the graving.[17] Likewise he received 13s. 6d. for engraving the arms on a cup and cover
presented to Magdalen College, Oxford, in the same year (Figure 98). Great Belling
Church, Northants, has a communion-flagon given also in 1697 by Lady O'Brian and
engraved with the sacred monogram, the arms of the donor and an inscription, for
which Rhodes received only 3s. 6d. The prices which he charged appear low but seem
to be in line with current rates. It is distressing, however, to find that when he tendered
his bill he had often to be content with a payment on account. He does not seem
to have found the custom of Sir Francis Child much more satisfactory since Child's
Bank has a pathetic note dated 20 August 1709, running as follows: 'I am putt to a strait,
pray lett my sonn[18] have tenn shillings and will infinitely oblige—yor Humb^{ble} Servt
Benj. Rhodes'. He was not in business in a small way since we can trace two of his

apprentices—William Starling[19] who was bound in 1688 and Benjamin Rhodes bound in 1694 who was probably a nephew.[20] When old age forced him to give up work he had recourse to a familiar expedient for raising cash by publishing a book of his designs. It was entitled:

A
NEW BOOK
of
CYPHERS

Containing in general all Names
Interwoven, & reversed, by Alphabet.
Being very pleasent for Gentlemen
and Ladys, and usefull for all sorts
of Artists, as Painters, Carvers, Engravers
Chacers, Watchmakers, Imbroderers &
With severall other usefull &
necessary, Examples with
Additions
Composed & Engraven
after the newest and true Mode by
BENJ. RHODES
Printed by T. Bickerton
for Theo. Sanders at ye
Bell in Little Britain
1723

Despite the claim that his work was in the 'newest and true Mode' it was in 1723 rather old fashioned. He did not reproduce any of his heraldic designs, but his ciphers are very much like those which he had been using at the end of the previous century. The fact that his book contains a plate with a carefully engraved royal crown and a florid double cipher of '*GR*' (Figure 99) suggests that he may have had some share of the work for the Jewel House, but no proof of this has come to light. There must survive a considerable number of examples of the work of Rhodes since he was working on his own for at least forty-five years. He must have supported himself entirely by engraving plate since he is not known to have worked for the printers. His heraldic cartouches are easily recognizable and when they are found on a piece with the mark of John Bodington, it is safe to claim them for him since, as we have seen, Hoare was a patron of that goldsmith.

There were, in fact, several better engravers decorating plate in the reigns of Anne and George I. The activities of the Rollos family is complicated by the fact that there was more than one member bearing the same christian name working at about the same

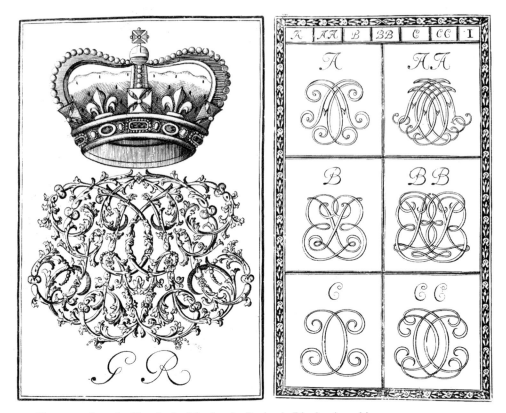

99. Two pages from the *New Book of Cyphers* by Benjamin Rhodes, issued in 1723
See page 85

time. Some appear to have been engravers whilst others were plate-workers. They were of foreign origin since the senior members of the family were granted denization, but it is not clear from which country they had come. Probably they worked as a team, the individual members specializing in different techniques. Philip Rollos I and his son Philip Rollos II were both plate-workers and served in subordinate capacity for the Jewel Office. They were both free of the Goldsmiths' Company but John Rollos was not. He described himself as engraver when binding his son Christian as apprentice to Philip Rollos II on 21 December 1721. His speciality was engraving seals and stamps. On 8 October 1707, the Stamp Office settled a bill including payment to Giles Quinn for cutting escutcheons and to John Rollos for engraving.[21] His connection with the Stamp Office lasted until his death on 16 May 1743, but since 1720 he had also been engraving seals for the Crown. George Vertue records that 'he gained a considerable fortune, whereby he left his sons or brother's relations about 200[li.] in Rents, Land or Money'.[22] We have no direct reference to him in connection with the engraving of plate but it seems likely that he also carried out this sort of work. For this reason I suggest

100. JOHN ROLLOS, attributed to
Detail of a gilt BASIN engraved with the arms of Queen Anne
1705 hallmark. Mark of Philip Rollos
Victoria and Albert Museum. See page 87

that he may have been responsible for engraving the arms of Queen Anne on the large basin (Figure 100), bearing the mark of Philip Rollos I and the hallmark for 1705, which formed part of the plate issued to Thomas Wentworth, Lord Raby, when he was appointed ambassador to the King of Prussia. If this attribution be accepted, it would apply also to other pieces bearing the marks of the two Rollos.

It is unfortunate that our main source of information about Joseph Sympson (or Simpson)[23] is Horace Walpole who habitually disparaged engravers on silver. He tells us that 'Joseph Simpson was very low in his profession, cutting arms on pewter plates, till, having studied in the academy, he was employed by Tillemans[24] on plate of Newmarket, to which he was permitted to put his name, and, which, though it did not please the painter, served to make Simpson known. He had a son of the same name, of whom he had conceived extraordinary hopes, but who died in 1736, without having attained much excellence.[25] The Newmarket racing trophy has not come to light but his

101. JOSEPH SYMPSON
Gilt SALVER engraved with the arms of Richard, fifth Viscount Ingram
1717 hallmark. Mark of William Lukin
Victoria and Albert Museum. See page 88

signed works are far from despicable and mostly have provenances connecting them with the most aristocratic houses. The earliest examples of his are heraldic decorations on a ewer and basin bearing the 1715 hallmark and the mark of William Lukin with whom he appears to have had a close relationship and who allows him to sign his work. His next signed piece is a gilt salver hallmarked 1717 (Figure 101) engraved in the

centre with the arms of Richard, fifth Viscount Ingram impaling those of his wife Lady Anne Howard whom he married in about 1717 and who died in April 1721 leaving no issue. The surround is treated in a most imaginative manner, having at the top the sun radiating upon figures of the Four Seasons who are contained within a framework of broken scrolls. At the bottom is a battle scene.[26]

Sir Robert Walpole was Chancellor of the Exchequer from October 1715 until April 1717 and again from April 1721 until the death of George I in June 1727, so that he would naturally have been entitled to convert to his own use the seal made obsolete on the accession of George II. Although Sir Robert chose to have the seal made into a salver, the engraved design broke right away from those which Gribelin had used on his salvers. The exact date cannot be established since it merely is stamped with the mark of Lukin. Above the representations of the two sides of the seal is Apollo in his chariot, whilst below is shown Victory flanked by captives and martial trophies.[27]

The next two examples of Sympson's work present the complication that they were engraved a considerable number of years after the date indicated by the hallmarks. An oval basin bearing the mark of Simon Margas and hallmark for 1718, is engraved with the arms of Francis Greville, seventh Earl Brooke, impaling those of his bride Elizabeth Hamilton whom he married in 1742. The other piece bears the mark of William Lukin but no hallmark and is a two-handled cup and cover[28] in a style fashionable around 1715. It is engraved with a fully developed rococo cartouche engraved with the arms of Thompson (London), impaling Cave, surrounded by scrolls, *amorini* and floral swags (Figure 102). The date of the marriage has not yet been discovered but the character of the design suggests the seventeen-forties. It is possible that both of these pieces were in the stock of William Lukin when Sympson engraved them. Other goldsmiths were not so indulgent over the matter of signatures and there must survive a number of other examples of Sympson's work. Caution must be exercised in making attributions since we are concerned with a period when a number of capable engravers were at work, the names of some of whom must be found listed in Appendix II, but whose work has not been identified. A number of pieces bearing the mark of Augustine Courtauld[29] seem to show the hand of Sympson and help to fill the gap between the earlier and later of his signed works. To these may be added the decoration of some pieces bearing the mark of Thomas Farren, particularly the very beautifully engraved salver with the 1733 hallmark showing the arms of John Shales Barrington (Figure 103) who was so proud of his royal descent.[30]

Paul de Lamerie built up, between 1713 and 1751, the largest silversmithing business which London saw in the eighteenth century. By the time that it had reached its fullest expansion, he was providing much work for the engravers. They were always competent, although by the time that he had become wedded to the rococo style they

103. JOSEPH SYMPSON, attributed to
Detail of SALVER engraved with the arms of John Shales Barrington
1733 hallmark. Mark of Thomas Farren
Victoria and Albert Museum. See page 90

90

104. Detail of CENTREPIECE. Arms of Sir Richard Newdegate, Bart., impaling those of his wife Sophia Conyers
1743 hallmark. Mark of Paul de Lamerie
Victoria and Albert Museum. See page 91

tended to produce heraldic cartouches showing little power of invention (Figure 104). Ellis Gamble was amongst the engravers whom he employed. He was the son of Robert Gamble, gentleman, of Plymouth,[31] who bound him apprentice in 1702 to Richard Hopthrow, Merchant Taylor, from whom he obtained his freedom in 1712. Although this rather long apprenticeship suggests impecuniosity, in the same year he married Elizabeth Smalbore and set up shop in Blue Cross Street, Leicester Fields. In 1713 he took on two apprentices, Stephen Fowler and William Hogarth. In 1717 he took as apprentice Felix Pellett, a Fleming, probably fearing that he might be short-handed when Hogarth's time expired. In January 1733 he was made bankrupt[32] but was sufficiently re-established by 1737 to take on as apprentice William Granville. The date of his death is not known.

By employing William Hogarth, his master did his own posthumous reputation untold harm. The controversy regarding Hogarth's engraving of plate may be divided into two parts. The first centres round the period of his apprenticeship and concerns a miscellaneous collection of book-plates, trade-cards etc. but also some pulls taken from plate put together by Samuel Ireland (d. 1800) who disposed of them three years before his death. They are now in the Print Room of the British Museum. These pulls were accepted by John Nichols in his *Biographical Anecdotes of William Hogarth* (1781), and by Horace Walpole whenever he failed to recognize that the print was really taken from a piece of plate. Amongst these are two which are clearly taken from salvers or waiters. The larger of these (Figure 105) shows an architectural composition with terms of the Four Seasons together with the arms of Antonio (Isaac) Suasso who married a member of the da Costa family.[33] The second (Figure 106) shows a similar design but has the

91

105 ELLIS GAMBLE, attributed to
Pull from a salver engraved with the
arms of Antonio Suasso. Perhaps
executed by Hogarth from his master's
design
British Museum. See page 91

106. ELLIS GAMBLE,
attributed to
Pull from a salver engraved
with the arms of Sir
Gregory Page, Bart. (d.
1720). Perhaps executed by
William Hogarth from his
master's design
British Museum. See page 91

107. Ellis Gamble, attributed
to
Detail of a TWO-HANDLED CUP.
Not executed by William
Hogarth
1719 hallmark. Mark of David
Willaume
*Messrs. S. J. Shrubsole, New
York. See page 94*

108. William Hogarth,
attributed to
Pull from a salver. 'The Rape of the
Lock'
About 1716
British Museum. See page 94

arms of Sir Gregory Page of Greenwich. He was a wealthy East India merchant who was created a baronet in 1714 but died in 1720.[34] Attempts to discredit Ireland's attributions to Hogarth stress that they are not at all in the style affected by the artist. This overlooks the fact that they date from the period of his apprenticeship when he was liable to be instructed to engrave his master's designs. Whilst attributing these designs to Gamble, it is possible to believe that Ireland was not entirely wrong. To Mr. Eric Shrubsole of New York I am indebted for drawing my attention to a two-handled cup bearing the 1719 hallmark and goldsmith's mark of David Willaume. It shows (Figure 107) a pair of terms of rather indeterminate sex, flanking a bust of Diana above a cartouche with a double cipher. It so closely resembles the two pulls which have just been described, that it seems quite safe to attribute it to Gamble's workshop. But there is no reason for claiming that Hogarth had any hand in its execution, which is not quite up to the standard of that on the two pulls, so that we may suspect that Gamble entrusted the engraving to one of his two other apprentices.[36]

We are left with the impression that Gamble was a very respectable artist but with rather restricted powers of invention. Those who have challenged Hogarth's connection with the pulls from the two salvers have argued that they are not at all in the style which we should expect the artist to choose. Perhaps we may trace Hogarth's real feeling about his master's designs in another pull (Figure 108) in the Ireland Collection. It is evidently taken from a salver although Nichols described it as a small oval print for 'The Rape of the Lock' for the top of a snuff-box. At the top is the initial 'B' with a coronet above. Below is a bust labelled 'BELINDA' above a cartouche with a double cipher of 'AP' and a scene of the incident which gave rise to the poem. On either side is a term having the initials 'W' and 'H' below the pedestal. At the bottom is a scroll inscribed with the two concluding lines of the poem:

This lock the Muse shall consecrate to fame,
And midst the stars inscribe Belinda's name.

Throughout, 'Belinda', Arabella Fermor, took Pope's poem in good heart so that it grew from two to five cantos. Lord Petre who had raped the lock in 1711, did not marry Arabella, but in 1716 she married Francis Perkins, owner of the picturesque Ufton Court near Aldermaston in Berkshire. The two pairs of turtle doves suggest that the salver was a wedding present to the heroine and explains the 'AP' in the cipher. The engraving need not be dismissed as being unworthy of Hogarth. It is a light-hearted affair to record an absurd incident. Since it was probably executed during his apprenticeship, it is likely that the work was done on the quiet as it manifestly makes a mockery of Gamble's art.

After completing his apprenticeship Hogarth decided to devote himself to other forms of art but there is nothing to suggest that he regarded the engraving of plate with revulsion. Whilst he was building up his reputation, it is unlikely that he would have

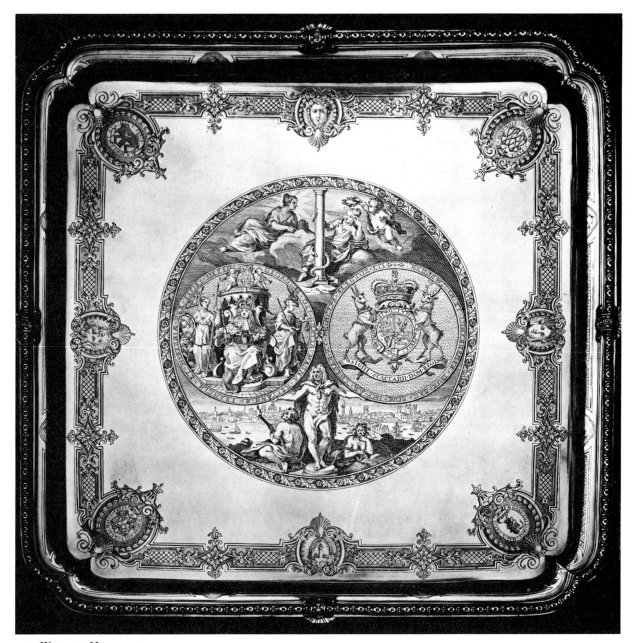

109. WILLIAM HOGARTH
THE WALPOLE SALVER, made from the Exchequer Seal of George I
1728 hallmark. Mark of Paul de Lamerie. W. $19\frac{1}{4}$ in (49 cm)
Victoria and Albert Museum. See page 96

refused important commissions from the leading goldsmith in London. The second seal salver made from an Exchequer Seal of George I bears the goldsmith's mark of Paul de Lamerie and the hallmark for 1728. It is usually referred to as the 'Walpole Salver' although the salver engraved by Joseph Sympson is equally entitled to be known by this name since both were made for Sir Robert Walpole. The attribution to Hogarth of the engraving on the 1728 salver has been much contested[38] but has quite a long history and is now widely accepted. Unlike the other Exchequer Seal salvers it is square and has a central roundel showing both sides of the seal supported by a figure of Hercules at whose feet sprawl figures of Calumny and Envy behind whom is a distant view of London. The two Cardinal Virtues not already shown on the obverse of the seal, recline on clouds at the top of the composition. Round the edge of the salver is an ornamental border broken by masks and with the arms, crest and cipher of Walpole in the corners. The first reference to Hogarth in connection with this piece occurs in Nichols's *Biographical Anecdotes*[39] in 1781, where he mentions amongst the engravings 'The Great Seal of England with a distant view of London, an impression from a large silver table'.[40] In the second edition, which appeared in the following year, he added 'This was given to Mr. S. Ireland by a Mr. Bonneau.'[41] When Samuel Ireland's collection was sold in 1797 the catalogue notes: 'The genuineness of this very scarce print admits no doubt. It was given to the proprietor by a Mr. Bonneau,[42] an intimate friend of Hogarth's with the assurance that it was engraved by him when an apprentice.' The statement that the salver was engraved whilst Hogarth was an apprentice is obviously untrue, since he must have been free for ten years and this discrepancy has been used to discredit the whole story. Though Samuel Ireland was wrong in claiming his print (now in the Royal Library at Windsor Castle) as unique, he had certainly got a scoop. A similar impression in the Print Room of the British Museum presents the peculiar feature that the royal arms above the king's head on the seal lacks the customary *Honi soit qui mal y pense*. This proves that it must have been taken before the salver left the engraver's workshop. The trump card of those who have impugned the Hogarth attribution is that there is no reference to the print nor the salver in Horace Walpole's *Catalogue of Mr. Hogarth's Prints* nor in either of the two editions of the *Anecdotes of Painting in England*. The challengers make the assumption that Walpole knew of the prints and that he inherited the two seal salvers direct from his father. He must have been only a child when the Sympson salver was delivered to his father's house,[43] whilst the present salver was produced in the year in which he was sent to Eton. Both salvers are in perfect condition so that he may not have set eyes upon them until he succeeded his unsatisfactory nephew as third Earl of Orford in 1791. He took no interest in contemporary silver and the salvers would only have been of value to him as memorials of his father.

The final argument against the Hogarth attribution has been that it was not in his style. This is countered by the nature of the order which demanded a formal style. If we ask

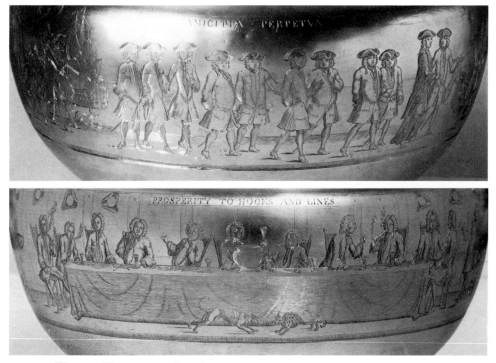

110, 111. WILLIAM HOGARTH, attributed to
Details from the TREBY PUNCH-BOWL
1723 hallmark. Mark of Paul de Lamerie
Ashmolean Museum, Oxford. See page 97

what was the sort of design which Hogarth liked to execute we get an inkling from the engraving on the Belinda salver (Figure 108). On the other hand, there does exist a piece which is engraved in exactly the style which Hogarth might be supposed to prefer. This is the punch-bowl bearing the mark of Paul de Lamerie with the hallmark for 1723 (Figures 110 and 111). It was made for George Treby, M.P. for Dartmouth, for presentation to Arthur Holdsworth, an alderman of that town. It commemorates the success of the local privateers and is engraved with a scene which is carried round the bowl. On one side is seen a procession of shareholders coming away from the ship, and above, 'AMICITIA PERPTVA'; whilst on the other is a long table at which the shareholders are seen, smoking and drinking below the inscription 'PROSPERITY TO HOOKS AND LINES'. Against the attribution is the fact that it was not claimed for Hogarth by either Ireland or Nichols, and we know that Lamerie had on his books other engravers capable of doing justice to genre subjects (page 107).

On 27 November 1740, the wardens decided that since the Goldsmiths' Company had emerged from a period of financial stringency, it was time to replace the plate which had been consigned to the melting-pot between 1667 and 1711. The orders were

112. CHARLES GARDNER
Detail of a gilt SALVER engraved with arms of the
Goldsmiths' Company
1741 hallmark. Mark of Thomas Farren
Goldsmiths' Company. See page 98

113. CHARLES GARDNER
Detail of a CASTER engraved with arms of the Goldsmiths'
Company
1740 hallmark. Mark of Richard Bayley
Goldsmiths' Company. See page 99

distributed between four leading members of the Court, Paul de Lamerie, Richard
Bayley, Thomas Farren and Humphrey Payne but it was stipulated that the engraving
should be done by Charles Gardner,[44] who was probably the most prosperous of the
silver-engravers who were free of the Company. Since he would seem to have confined
himself entirely to engraving plate, he is not mentioned by Walpole. He had been
apprenticed to William Starling II on 17 September 1705, and became a freeman of the
Goldsmiths' Company in 1714. Eleven apprentices were bound to him between 1714
and 1744, and he appears to have had three working for him for most of the time,
although most prosperous engravers managed with two. He became a liveryman in
1721. No signed works have yet been found and we can only judge him by the engraving
on the pieces included in the Goldsmiths' order of 1740. These may be presumed to
give a fair sample of his work although probably he was only personally involved with
the more important pieces, entrusting the rest to the staff of his workshop. We may
credit him, therefore, with the engraving of the arms on the two salvers (called tea-
tables in the records) bearing the mark of Thomas Farren (Figure 112). The central
roundels are in the magnificent style and though the cartouches are framed by scrolls,
the effect is entirely balanced. The naturalistic rendering of the heraldic beasts (albeit
monsters) and the meticulous hatching of the colours foreshadow the fashions of the
Regency and Victorian periods. Although in these respects Gardner was ahead of his

time, this need not be taken as a compliment. His weaknesses are seen in the engraving of the lesser pieces, doubtless executed by his apprentices, such as that on the sugar-caster (Figure 113) belonging to the Warwick frame and the half-pint mugs made by Richard Bayley, and the 'tea-waiters' made by Humphrey Payne. Eventually payment of £29. 14s. 0d. was made to Gardner 'for graving great part of the said plate'.

By 1740 Gardner had been at work for a quarter of a century so that much of his work must survive. Allowance must, however, be made for an artist's style to evolve over the years. The most revealing feature appears to be the stiff and formal rendering of his heraldry and for this reason is ascribed the engraving of the arms of Henry Somerset, third Duke of Beaufort, on the bottom of a jewel-casket made by John White in 1729 (Figure 114). The ornamental border is clearly taken from some copy-book and does not suggest that he was experimenting with the rococo. At present it is not possible to compile an 'opus' for him.

The case of Charles Gardner is not unique since there were active at this time a number of highly skilled engravers whose identities cannot be established. Who, for instance, engraved the plateau (Figure 115) for the centrepiece made by George Wickes in 1745 for Frederick, Prince of Wales? We only know that Wickes charged £23. 16s. 0d. for the engraving.[45] He would appear to have been the same artist who engraved the arms on

114. CHARLES GARDNER, attributed to
BOTTOM OF A JEWEL-CASKET engraved with arms of third Duke of Beaufort
1729 hallmark. Mark of John White
Colonial Williamsburg. See page 99

115. PLATEAU, gilt, engraved with arms of Frederick, Prince of Wales
1745 hallmark. Mark of George Wickes
Buckingham Palace, by gracious permission of H.M. the Queen. See page 99

the Prince's punch-bowl made by Wickes in 1750[46] and also for the latter's trade-card.[47] The Prince was an important customer who had to be given the best work even though he was poor at settling his accounts.

In general the top goldsmiths had each a favourite engraver to whom they passed the more important orders, leaving the more routine work to lesser workers. Thus we have seen that William Lukin's best orders went to Joseph Sympson. We have also noted how Lamerie distributed his more selective work, but he had also others to do the more repetitive engraving. The Newdegate centrepiece of 1743 is distinguished by reason of its silversmithing and it must have seemed superfluous to employ a first-class engraver for the five versions of the arms of Sir Richard Newdegate and his wife (Figure 104). By the middle of the century there was a scarcity of young first-class engravers although there were still plenty who could not make the grade. Amongst these, known to us only because of a signature, was Benjamin Levi of Portsmouth,[48] who engraved a two-handled cup made by Richard Bayley and hallmarked in 1741. It was engraved for presentation in 1743 to Richard Hawkes, Beaconer of King's Lynn. The upper part of the bowl shows the arms of the recipient on a rococo cartouche flanked by figures of Neptune and of a merman (Figure 116); below is a poem telling how the fenland was protected by the defences raised to repel the attacks of 'stern Neptune's Rage & Boreas' Spleen'. It is a feeble production as might be expected of a craftsman who was only an all-round jobbing engraver as is shown by his trade-card which states that he engraved

116. BENJAMIN LEVI
Detail of TWO-HANDLED CUP
engraved with arms of Richard
Hawkes
1741 hallmark. Mark of
Richard Bayley
*King's Lynn Museum. See page
101*

seals, stamps, plate, copperplate and pewter 'at the corner of Union Row, in Queen Street on Portsmouth Common'. He was a member of a family of engravers and his son Jacob will be mentioned later.

Although silver decorated in the Chinese taste was popular during the rococo period, the ornament was nearly always either cast or embossed. Engraved chinoiserie is quite rare. We have no certain clue as to the decorator of the large salver engraved with the arms of Douglas within a chinoiserie surround (Figure 117) and with the mark of William Cripps and the 1758 hallmark, but it may well have been the engraver of an elaborate chinoiserie rococo trade-card of Edward Dobson which must have been produced about this date and which is signed 'Brooke fecit Fleet Street'.[49] I have not been able to trace him.

The latest signed engraving in the rococo style is upon a salver bearing the mark of Samuel Courtauld the elder and hallmark for 1763 (Figure 118). It shows a composition of three coats-of-arms on rococo cartouches, one resting against a figure of Justice, another by an eagle, and the third backed by a ruined castle. Below is a floral swag and *J. Teasdale F.* Nothing is known of him but it is possible that he was related to William Teasdale who received the freedom of the Goldsmiths' Company in 1751.

The themes engraved on plate between 1700 and 1765 were predominantly armorial but this left the artists considerable scope for purely decorative surrounds. Of the unheraldic subjects there are only two important religious examples. One is 'The

117. SALVER engraved with arms of Douglas
(perhaps re-engraved)
1758 hallmark. Mark of William Cripps. D. 25 in
(63.5 cm)
Collection of the late Mrs. Ionides. See page 101

118. J. TEASDALE
Detail of SALVER
1763 hallmark. Mark of Samuel Courtauld
Messrs. Thomas Lumley. See page 101

119. Detail of ALTAR-DISH, gilt.
'The Last Supper'
1750 hallmark. Mark of John Payne
St. Lawrence Jewry. See page 105

120. ALMS-DISH. View of Elmham
Church
1707 hallmark. Mark of John East
Elmham Church, Norfolk. See page 105

121. THE CUMBERLAND TANKARD engraved with scenes of the battle of Culloden
1746 hallmark. Mark of Gabriel Sleath. H. 12¾ in (32·5 cm)
National Army Museum. See page 105

Deposition' engraved by Simon Gribelin in 1706 on the altar-dish for the chapel at Dunham Massey (Figure 90) and the other 'The Last Supper' on the altar-dish with the mark of John Penn at St. Lawrence Jewry (Figure 119). Topographical subjects are no less rare and range in quality from the deplorable representation of Elmham Church, evidently by a local artist (Figure 120), on an alms-dish bearing the mark of John East and hallmark for 1707, to the highly sophisticated panorama of the City of London on the Walpole Salver (Figure 109).

The representation of naval and military subjects was a fresh development. The earliest example noted is a tankard made by Edward Cornock with the hallmark for 1713 but engraved with a scene of the storming of Namur in 1695.[50] Next comes the massive tankard made by Gabriel Sleath in 1746, engraved with a detailed scene of the battle of Culloden (Figure 121) and intended for presentation to the Duke of Cumberland. The

122. SALVER engraved with 'Exploits of H.M.S. Tartar'
1757 hallmark. Mark of Alexander Johnston. D. 27 in (69 cm)
Inverness Museum, on loan from Bruce Corporation. See page 106

105

123. TOBACCO-BOX. Subject adapted from an engraving by Pierre Bourdon
1718 hallmark. Mark of Edward Cornock. W. $3\frac{7}{8}$ in (10 cm)
Colonial Williamsburg. See page 107

engraving is crude and may have embarrassed the duke who, although not a silver specialist like his brother the Prince of Wales, is credited with more taste than humanity. Nautical subjects fared much better. It became quite usual for the owners or the insurers to present a piece of plate (teapot, waiter or salver) to the captain who had saved his ship by good seamanship or from capture by privateers. Sometimes one ship is depicted or else two ships fighting. By far the most important example is a splendid salver (Figure 122), bearing the mark of Alexander Johnston and hallmark for 1757, engraved with a scene with ships in front of a town, having above the recipient's arms and below a scroll inscribed: 'Presented by the Two Assurance Companys and Merchants of London to John Lockhart Esqr Captain of his Majesty's ship TARTAR for his Gallant Service in protecting the Trade of the Nation by taking many French Privateers in the years 1756–7.'

There was no spectacular increase in the engraving of genre subjects but the standard of execution had much improved. The most important example is the Lamerie punch-bowl (Figures 110 and 111), engraved with the members of an association of owners of a privateer, which has already been tentatively ascribed to Hogarth. A much less plausible attribution to the artist has been made on behalf of a snuff-box engraved with a meeting of the members of the Spectator Club as described in Volume I, No. 2 issued in 1711, but the scene is depicted within a rococo frame and must have been executed much later.[51] A tobacco-box, made by Edward Cornock and hallmarked in 1718, is engraved with a young man seated on a chair, holding a wineglass in his right hand whilst smoking a long pipe held in his left. He is surrounded by floral scrolls (Figure 123). Mr. John Davis discovered that the man was copied from a book of designs published in 1703 in Paris by Pierre Bourdon.[52] The adaptation has not been very skilfully done since in the original the young man, evidently an author who has run out of inspiration, rests his right arm on a table on which is a scroll, ruler and penknife. Two further genre engravings, both of excellent quality, deserve mention. One is upon a set of four tumblers with the mark of Aymé Videau and hallmark for 1743, each engraved with a sentimental subject probably from a French novel, framed in very elaborate rococo tracery.[53] The other is also on a tumbler but with the mark of Lamerie and hallmark for 1741 and is engraved on one side with St. George and the dragon and the other with two duellists and a scroll inscribed 'Uffington Castle Berks' and 'A–N', 1741.[54]

Notes

1. All the references to Lemuel King date before 1700, so that although he pioneered in the new style we were forced to include him in the last chapter.
2. *Anecdotes*, p. 454.
3. No. 1859/6/25, acquired at Sotheby's in 1859 but undoubtedly the volume which Walpole mentions as being in his possession.
4. Museum No. M. 307 1962. Width 3⅜ in (8.5 cm).
5. Because of the small scale and also the inscriptions being in reverse, the following full description is given: 1. At top, Venus in her chariot drawn by doves above which is Cupid ('QUI PEUT LUY RESISTER'). 2. Venus with three attendants, admiring herself in a mirror ('SEULLES DIGNES DE LA SERVIR'). 3. The Judgement of Paris ('A LA PLUS BELLE'). 4. Cupid led by a dog on a lead ('LA FIDELITE ME CONDIUT').
6. T. Blount, *Glossographia*, 1661.
7. Gribelin's engraving is found mainly upon pieces bearing the Britannia hallmark, but in the possession of the City of Westminster is a very handsome dish stamped with a double monogram goldsmith's mark which would have gone out of use on 27 March 1697.
8. A. J. Collins (*Jewels and Plate of Queen Elizabeth I*, pp. 95–7) has shown that the custom of allowing the silver of a seal which had become obsolete (e.g. by the death of the sovereign or a change in his title) to become the perquisite of the holder, who might make it into a piece of plate, dates from the fifteenth century. There does not appear to be a fixed rule as to which offices qualified for this practice.
9. Another peculiar feature about this salver is that it has a twin bearing the mark of David Willaume and hallmark for 1726, by which date the Earl of Halifax had been dead for nine years. Both salvers had been in the collection of the Duke of Sussex (Christie's, 24 June 1843, Lots 444–5). The second is now the property of the Society of the Inner Temple.
10. Two are in the Victoria and Albert Museum and the two others in the Museum of Fine Arts, Boston. Another, made in the same year by the same goldsmith, differs by having a plain rim instead of the elaborately chased design in the style of Stephano della Bella. It is in the Royal Ontario Museum, Toronto.
11. It is sad to note that Sir Benjamin died only four years later.

12. Samuel was to be employed to 'draw prospects'.

13. H. P. Hoare, *Hoare's Bank, a Record 1655–1955*, 1955.

14. e.g. Admiral Russell, who was a good customer of Hoare's; when he became Earl of Orford, he returned a dozen plates to have a coronet added. For this Rhodes received 6s.

15. This means that he took a pull from the engraving and whilst the ink was still wet used it to make a print in the account-book. Though a counter-proof inevitably lacks quality, it at any rate shows the arms the right way round.

16. The dukes of Beaufort, Newcastle and Queensberry, the earls of Ashburnham, Derby, Godolphin, Montagu and Northumberland.

17. The two coats-of-arms appear on opposite sides of the cup.

18. Nothing is known of him.

19. Later to be the master of Charles Gardner.

20. Son of Samuel Rhodes of Flitwick, Bedfordshire. He never took up his freedom and his fate is unknown.

21. *Calendar of Treasury Books*, XXI, pt. 2, p. 437.

22. *Walpole Society*, 1933, III, p. 115; 1937, V, p. 48.

23. In 1726 was published a mediocre work entitled *A New Book of Cyphers* by Samuel Sympson who was probably a relation.

24. Born at Antwerp and came to England in 1708 and specialized in topographical and racing subjects. Died in 1734.

25. *Anecdotes*, p. 458.

26. Although Viscount Ingram held a commission in the army there is no record of his ever having gone into action.

27. Illustrated in *Apollo*, LXV, 1957, p. 286.

28. An illustration ot the whole piece appears in the *Catalogue of the Elizabeth B. Miles Collection* at the Wadsworth Atheneum. I must thank the author and owner of this collection and also Mr. Eric Shrubsole for putting me in touch with this piece.

29. For instance J. F. Hayward, *The Courtauld Silver*, 1975, Plates 15, 17 and 18; also a salver with the mark of Augustine Courtauld sold at the Parke-Bernet Galleries, New York, on 20 March 1970.

30. He was descended from George, Duke of Clarence, brother of Edward IV and Isabella Neville, daughter of Warwick the Kingmaker.

31. Apparently no relation of William Gamble, Goldsmith.

32. According to William Le Hardy on the petition of Paul de Lamerie, but neither Ronald Paulson (*Hogarth, His Life and Times*, 1971, p. 45) nor I have found any authority for this detail. The bankruptcy is reported in the *London Gazette* for 2–6 January 1732–3 and 17 February.

33. The arms would also fit Antonio's father, Francisco Lopez who had also married a da Costa, but he had died in 1710.

34. According to Nichols, 'at Sir Gregory's sale, the table was purchased by Mr. Morrison, who after taking off twenty-five impressions, melted the plate' (*Hogarth's Works* by John Ireland and John Nichols, III, p. 318).

35. The date when Hogarth completed his apprenticeship is not known. As he had been apprenticed in 1712 he may only have become free in 1719.

36. There are two further pulls in the Ireland collection which are clearly taken from pieces of plate. One shows a section of the engraved border of a waiter. The other is described by Nichols as 'A coat-of-arms with two slaves and trophies, plate for books.' Since the motto 'CRESCENT' is in reverse, it is clearly from the lid of a tobacco-box. The arms are those of a second son of the family of Tatton, County Chester. Both of these reflect Gamble's rather than Hogarth's taste.

37. It is not clear how Walpole became entitled to the silver of two Exchequer Seals but I was informed by Mr. Roger Ellis of the Public Record Office, that seals were sometimes scrapped for no apparent reason. The present salver would seem to have been made out of the seal in use from 1724 until the end of the reign, an impression of which is in the British Museum. The Sympson salver must commemorate an earlier seal. both seals appeared in the belated sale of the Strawberry Hill Collection in 1842 as Lots 115 and 120 on the eleventh day.

38. By P. A. S. Phillips in *Life and Times of Paul de Lamerie*, 1935, pp. 86–90; A. J. Collins in *Jewels and*

Plate of Queen Elizabeth I, 1955, p.97n. Both writers, whilst discounting the attribution to Hogarth because of the unlikeness to his style, make no allowance for the possibility that when confronted with a task which demanded a strictly classical treatment, he may have sought help from his father-in-law Sir James Thornhill who was a master of it.

39. p. 148.

40. 'Table' at this period meant a salver. This reference makes it clear that Nichols and Ireland knew that there must be a salver but did not know where it was. This was only cleared up when both seal salvers appeared in the Strawberry Hill sale in 1842.

41. p. 345.

42. 'Mr. Bonneau' may have been either a fashionable drawing-master who died in 1786, or else one of the five children of Pierre Bonneau, engraver of Rennes, who escaped from France in 1687 and abjured Catholicism in Jersey.

43. This might account for his mis-spelling Joseph Sympson's name as 'Simpson'.

44. Court Minutes, 13, p. 380. Presumably Lamerie found his own engraver for the crest and arms on the wardens' standish. These are finely executed in the full rococo style which was favoured by Lamerie but not, as far as we know by Gardner.

45. Arthur Grimwade, 'The Garrard Ledgers' in *Proceedings of the Society of Silver Collectors*, I, 1961, p.8.

46. Victoria and Albert Museum, No. M. 10–1964.

47. A. Heal, *The London Goldsmiths 1200–1800*, 1935. Plate LXXVI.

48. He was the son of Jacob Levi of Wiesbaden. His tombstone still survives according to Cecil Roth in *Jewish Historical Society*, XIII, 1932–5, pp.161–2.

49. Heal, Plate XXIII.

50. Formerly in the Farrer Collection (E. A. Jones, *Farrer*, Plate XX).

51. It is not hallmarked and it is in the Victoria and Albert Museum, No. M. 53–1959. Maker's mark *RG (gothic)* unidentified.

52. John Davis, *English Silver at Williamsburg*, 1976, pp.207–8.

53. Grimwade, *Rococo*, p.67, Plate 92.

54. Museum of Fine Arts, Houston, *Silver by Paul de Lamerie in America*, 1956, No. 41. Uffington Castle is an early earthwork where it would be possible to arrange a duel without fear of interference.

Chapter V

1766 to 1805

Around the middle of the eighteenth century it became quite common for the register of apprentices at Goldsmiths' Hall to note that the candidate was being bound to a master specifically to learn engraving. The fact that the Goldsmiths' Company had come to recognize the engravers of silver as a separate craft, does not make our task very much easier since many of those who engraved plate continued to be registered with other companies and to work also for the printers and publishers. Although the Goldsmiths' records provide the names of many engravers it remains difficult to attach them to their work because of the lack of signatures. The greater number of names does not represent an increase in the demand for their services but rather the reverse. Silver-engraving has had its waves of popularity and the second half of the eighteenth century was a period of recession just as the fourteenth century had been. Several causes contributed to this. The simpler forms of the Adam style did not lend themselves to engraved decoration as well as the earlier ones had done—much of the earlier engraved work had been heraldic and it was difficult to combine forms essentially gothic with those based on classical art. Attempts were made time and again but the results were never really satisfactory as may be seen in the favourable examples chosen for illustration (Figures 126 and 135). The engravers were seldom afforded opportunities for heroic efforts and when they were allowed an all-over decoration, it was usually on a small scale. This tendency is admirably illustrated by two tea-caddies of which the earlier (Figure 124), bearing the mark of Pierre Gillois and hallmark for 1768, is decorated with an all-over floral trellis design obviously adapted from a textile pattern-book, whilst the other (Figure 125), with the mark of Augustin Le Sage and hallmark for 1777, shows classical ornament as understood by those who prepared designs for watch-case makers and jewellers. A salver (Figure 126), with the mark of Ebenezer Coker and hallmark for 1770, was deocrated by a more adventurous artist. The arms and surround are, indeed, not adventurous but the border of floral swags hung from the mouths of lions, goats, horses and oxen enclose little classical urns clearly borrowed

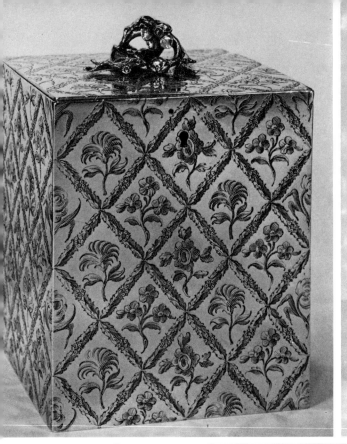

124. TEA-CADDY, gilt
1768 hallmark. Mark of Pierre
Gillois. H. 5 in (13 cm)
Victoria and Albert Museum. See
page 110

125. TEA-CADDY, gilt
1777 hallmark. Mark of Augustin
Le Sage. H. 4½ in (11·5 cm)
Victoria and Albert Museum. See
page 110

126. SALVER
1770 hallmark. Mark of Ebenezer
Coker. W. 16½ in (41·5 cm)
Messrs. Christie. See page 110

from some architectural work.[1] The floral swags are here engraved in the traditional manner and are not 'bright-cut' like most of those which decorate plate made in the last quarter of the century.

'Bright-cut' engraving made its appearance around 1775 and the novelty of its reflecting facets won it immediate popularity. Although the designs are vaguely classical, they cannot be described as scholarly. All the provincial centres succumbed to the new style and when we read of apprentices bound 'to learn engraving' we may imagine that many of them must have been set to do bright-cut. There was plenty of low-grade work to be done since it became fashionable to decorate minor pieces like teaspoons and mustard-pots which previously only carried crests or initials. There were, of course, varying degrees of proficiency in executing this type of engraving but especially high quality work is found on the plate bearing the mark of Robert Hennell I

127. ROBERT HENNELL II
ÉPERGNE
1785 hallmark. Mark of Robert Hennell II
Private collection. See page 113

(1741–1811).[2] Much of it may be credited to his nephew Robert Hennell II (1763–1832) to whose hand may be due the decoration of the handsome épergne of 1785 (Figure 127) shortly before he emerged from apprenticeship to his uncle to whom he had been bound in 1778. He was, in fact, exceptionally qualified since besides his training as a silversmith under his uncle, he had been also apprenticed to John Houle, engraver, who was not free of the Goldsmiths' Company although he entered a mark as a plate-worker at a much later date. Robert II seems to have been put in charge of the engraving at Hennells but seems also to have worked for other firms. In 1808 he set up in partnership with Henry Nutting, but this did not last for long. For the rest of his career he worked on his own and had his own mark of *RH in an oblong*.

There can be no doubt of the attractiveness of bright-cut which could add a little distinction to an otherwise dull piece, but the technique was over-employed and became monotonous. It had passed the peak of its popularity by 1800 but was still in use in Victorian times.

The Romantic movement was responsible for some of the most attractive engraving of this period but, as in the case of the Elizabethan engraved dishes, it is easier to trace the sources of the subjects than the actual engraver. A good example of this is a teapot with the mark of Francis Crump and hallmark for 1772 (Figures 128 and 129). The drum is engraved with two scenes and the lid shows demi-figures of the Four Seasons. One side of the drum (Figure 128) is engraved with a scene taken from *The Decameron*, fifth day, first novella; the other (Figure 129) has one taken from La Fontaine's *Contes et Nouvelles* which, with the title 'L'Hermite', recounts in verse a story derived from *The Decameron*, fourth day, second novella.[3] Both subjects are depicted with such fidelity as to make the identifications certain. Fashions in reading change but at the time that the teapot was engraved the subjects would not have appeared excessively obscure. It is not as yet possible to identify the sources from which the scenes were copied; the theme of both appears to be merely 'Beware of men.'

There is even less link between the subjects engraved on the back and front of a tobacco-box bearing the mark of John Deacon and hallmark for 1797. On the front (Figure 130) is engraved a scene of a maiden talking to her mother who is seated at a spinning wheel. On the end is inscribed: 'For in the wanderings of a vale etc' and 'Edw. & Emma'. It is, in fact, adapted from an illustration by James Heath, A.R.A. (1757–1834) for Cooke's edition of the poems of David Mallet published in 1795. On the bottom (Figure 131) is engraved the scene of Autolycus, Clown and Mopsa taken from *The Winter's Tale*, Act IV, Scene iii, and copied from the edition of Shakespeare's works published by T. Lowndes and Partners in 1783, where the engraving is credited to Michael Angelo Rooker, A.R.A. (1743–1801). The engraver does not seem to have had any scruple about making copies of the work of two living artists but this may be explained by the fact that the box was intended to remain in the possession of his family. Walter Jackson was apprenticed to John Thompson in 1793 and became free in 1801.

114

128, 129. TEAPOT engraved with scenes from *The Decameron*
1772 hallmark. Mark of Francis Crump. H. 4½ in (11·5 cm)
Sterling and Francine Clark Institute, Williamstown, Massachusetts. See page 113

130, 131. WALTER JACKSON
TOBACCO-BOX engraved with 'Edwin and Emma' and 'Autolycus'
1797 hallmark. Mark of John Deacon. H. 5½ in (14 cm)
Victoria and Albert Museum. See page 113

He was the son of John Jackson, printer, of Plough Court, Fetter Lane, to whom he presented the box. John Jackson returned the gift shortly before his death in 1802, after which it remained in the possession of his descendants until it was acquired for the Victoria and Albert Museum in 1911, together with the information that Walter Jackson had engraved silver for George III and the Prince Regent. Though the box was an eminently suitable gift for an engraver son to a printer father, it gives no evidence of any inventive capacity. Walter Jackson, however, became quite an important person in the trade and will be mentioned again later.

In 1713 Henry Monck, barber-surgeon, presented a horn tobacco-box for use at

115

132, 133. PAIR OF DISHES, gilt, engraved with mermen and bacchanals
1792 hallmark. Mark of William Sumner. D. 9½ in (24·5 cm)
Messrs. Thomas Lumley. See page 116

meetings of the Overseers of the Poor of the parishes of St. Margaret and St. John, Westminster. It is not clear why great sentiment got attached to the gift (which had cost 4d.) and led to it becoming a fetish. After the original box had been mounted in silver, it became customary for the overseers to provide a larger silver box into which it could be placed. These cases were engraved with the names of the successive overseers but also with a topical subject of either local or national interest. Thus the second case, which was in use from 1783–90, is engraved with a scene of the overseers seated at a table interviewing the poor. Its successor, which was in use from 1791–1808, is octagonal and covered with plaques ranging in subject from heads of Pitt and Fox to the battle of the Nile in 1798, to a sermon given in Westminster Hall to the volunteers in 1803, and the battle of Trafalgar in 1805. These plaques bear the mark of Peter, Ann and William Bateman but there is no indication of the identity of the engraver who was evidently well trained in book illustration.[4]

Since subjects borrowed from classical art were rarely used at this period, a pair of gilt dishes bearing the mark of William Sumner and hallmark for 1792 are somewhat exceptional. One (Figure 132) is engraved with two mermen fighting over a mermaid, whilst the other (Figure 133) shows two infant bacchanals. Both subjects look as if they had been copied from tailpieces in some book.

The date chosen for closing this chapter bisects the careers of two provincial engravers. The less important is Jacob Levi (d. 1816) son of Benjamin Levi who had engraved the cup for King's Lynn in 1741. His only identified work is a portrait of the Chief Rabbi Solomon Hirschel[5] which appears on a cup hallmarked 1809 (Figure 134), together with a lengthy Hebrew inscription about the occasions when wine-drinking is appropriate. Since Levi had been born in 1746 there must be earlier examples of his work.

Thomas Bewick of Newcastle is by far the most fully documented of all the artists who have engraved English silver, since we have not only the memoir which he wrote between the years 1822 and 1828 but also the account-books detailing the work executed for the Newcastle firm of Langlands and Robertson which supply a lot of interesting information including identifications of surviving pieces. The only region where uncertainty remains is in separating his earlier work from that of his master Ralph Beilby to whom he was apprenticed on 1 October 1767. Bewick was the son of a small farmer and mine-owner, and had not been brought up in an artistic environment but had discovered and developed a talent for the graphic arts. Ralph Beilby, on the

134. JACOB LEVI OF PORTSMOUTH BOWL OF A CUP engraved with portrait of Chief Rabbi Solomon Hirschel
1809 hallmark. Mark of Hyam Hyams
Jewish Museum. See page 116

other hand belonged to a highly artistic family. His father had been a jeweller and silversmith in Durham, but had failed and died in 1765. Three of Ralph's brothers and a sister had taken to designing or crafts of one sort or another. By the time that Bewick appeared on the scene they were established in Newcastle where they were building up a reputation for such divers skills as seal-cutting, enamelling and engraving glass, and engraving both for printers and silversmiths. Bewick must have learnt to engrave silver before he completed his apprenticeship in 1774. After a prolonged *wanderjahr* during which he made a tour of Scotland, he went on to London where he was able to obtain some insight into local trading conditions. In June 1777 he was back in Newcastle and was offered a partnership by his former master.

In 1953 the Laing Art Gallery, Newcastle, was presented with the Bewick account-books from which it is possible to glean much information regarding the dealings of Beilby and Bewick with the local silversmiths but especially with the important firm of

Langlands and Robertson.[6] The set of account-books is not complete but it covers both the period of Bewick's apprenticeship and of his partnership with Beilby, which was wound up at the end of 1797. After the beginning of the nineteenth century the series peters out, which is unfortunate since some of the most characteristic examples of Bewick's work date from his later years. The account-books are most enlightening with regard to the relationship between the engravers and the silversmiths. The first surprise is the considerable amount of work which is recorded. The porter from Langlands and Robertson appears to have been sent round three or four times a month, with a package of wares to be engraved. Most of it was, of course, trivial. Sometimes it included posies for rings or names on dog-collars. No indication is provided of the owner of a crest or of a coat-of-arms which had to be engraved. The charge for engraving a crest on a coffee-pot or a tankard was usually 4s. 6d. or 5s. Arms were more expensive.[7] On 22 November 1768 Beilby charged £1. 1s. 0d. for two coats-of-arms and a motto on a flagon. The heraldry on plate bearing the mark of Langlands and Robertson is not very vigorous and it is obvious that Beilby and Bewick did not make it a speciality. A scrap-book purporting to have formed part of the Bewick remains is in the Laing Art Gallery and contains book-plates and a few pulls of engraving on plate. The book-plates were probably provided by customers in order to ensure that the engraver should not make a mistake. In 1780 bright-cut engraving begins to be

135, 136. RALPH BEILBY
FREEDOM-BOX of Admiral Keppel
1779 Newcastle hallmark. Mark of Langlands and Robertson
Messrs. Sotheby. See page 119

mentioned. It was rather expensive as may be gathered from an entry, 'Mar. 9 Bright graving a Tea Pot with borders, Festoons etc. 12s.' According to Bewick his partner 'undertook the engraving of arms, crests and cyphers, on silver and every type of job for the silversmiths . . . but what he excelled in was ornamental silver engraving. In this, as far as I am able to judge, he was one of the best in the kingdom.'[8] If this last phrase be considered to refer to bright-cut engraving it may be deserved but much of the silver sold by Langlands and Robertson is by no means outstanding. It seems fair to attribute to Ralph Beilby the engraving on the freedom-box presented in 1779 to Admiral Keppel and for which £2. 2s. 2d. was charged in the account-book. On the bottom are the arms of the Newcastle Trinity House (Figure 135) whilst inside the lid is a scene of Neptune presenting the admiral to Britannia (Figure 136). It is likely that Beilby may also have engraved some of the presentation plate which grateful owners or insurers gave to captains who had brought their ships safely into port after alarming storms or

137. RALPH BEILBY or THOMAS BEWICK (?)
Detail of SALVER
1781 hallmark. Mark of Robert James
Messrs. Spink. See page 119

misadventures.[9] A typical example is a salver engraved with a brig surrounded by 'The Gift of the Underwriters in Sunderland to Alex^r & Jane Cunningham Tynemouth 1781' (Figure 137). Since the salver was made by Robert James and bears the London hallmark for 1781, it cannot be traced in the account-books. Bewick did not escape this type of work in which he was unable to display his own peculiar talents. A cake-basket in the museum at Lloyds is engraved with a ship billowing smoke and the inscription: 'A gift from the Unanimous and Equitable Associated Underwriters to Nich^s Fairless Esqr. for his intrepid Conduct and animated Example shewn in extinguishing the Fire on board the ship Joseph and Mary at South Shields on 7th Sept. 1798.' It is virtually certain that the engraving must have been done by Bewick since the partnership with Beilby lapsed at the end of this year.

Whilst it is usually difficult to distinguish the work of Bewick from that of Beilby when rendering nautical subjects, this does not extend to ones in which he was able to display

138. THOMAS BEWICK
Front of COMMUNION-FLAGON
1774 Newcastle hallmark. Mark of Langlands and Robertson
St. Andrew's Church, Newcastle (on loan to Laing Art Gallery). See page 120

his knowledge of the countryside. The earliest pieces attributable to him are to be found on a set of altar-plate provided for St. Andrew's Church, Newcastle. This consists of a pair of flagons with the mark of Langlands and Robertson and Newcastle hallmark for 1774, followed by a large alms-dish made by the same firm in 1784 and, finally, a pair of plates with the mark of Robert Pinkney and Robert Scott and Newcastle hallmark for 1787. Each piece is engraved with a wind-swept Northumbrian landscape in which the saint is seen leaning against his cross, with a small catch of fishes in front of him and his drying nets at one side (Figure 138).[10]

The account-books are much less informative about Bewick's engraving on silver after he had parted from Beilby. It was not a side of his business to which he attributed much importance, as his heart was really in wood-engraving and natural history. These major

139. THOMAS BEWICK
Detail of SALVER. 'The Harleston Hunt'
1808 Newcastle hallmark. Mark of Anne Robertson
Victoria and Albert Museum. See page 121

interests, however, were sometimes responsible for bringing him orders for engraving plate. His attitude towards hunting and shooting was ambiguous. Basically humanitarian, he obtained much help from local landowners and army officers whilst collecting material for his *General History of Quadrupeds* (1790) and *History of British Birds* (1797–1804). The illustrations in these works brought him into contact with a class of customer with which he would not ordinarily be associated. Thus a salver at the Victoria and Albert Museum (Figure 139) is engraved with a hunting scene and the inscription 'Presented by the Gentlemen of the Harleston Hunt to Mr. Dewing of Guist, March, 1808.'[11] It bears the Newcastle hallmark for this year and the mark of Anne Robertson and is recorded in the account-book as 'H. Hewitson Esqr. for Mr Dewing's Wa[i]ter £3. 13. 6.' It is a long way from Newcastle to Harleston in Norfolk, and it is not clear who was responsible for directing the order. Another salver is engraved with a meet of a hunt in front of a country house which has been identified as Burton Constable Hall, near Hull, but since a second-hand piece of 1733 was used, it cannot be exactly dated. Probably more examples will appear since it was only about thirty years ago that his achievements as an engraver of silver began to be realised.[12] His work stands very much alone and cannot be conveniently fitted into either the Adam or the Regency styles.

Notes

1. For a similar example with the mark of the same goldsmith but 1772 hallmark see Sotheby, 18 May 1967, Lot 61.

2. The main authority for the Hennell family is an article by Percy Hennell in *The Connoisseur*, February 1973, but he missed Robert II's apprenticeship to Houle which was discovered by Grimwade (op. cit., pp. 544 and 522).

3. I must record my thanks to Mr. Ketteridge of the Sterling and Francine Clark Art Institute, Williamstown, Mass., for providing the identifications. Figure 128 shows Cimon discovering Iphigenia resting in the middle of the day. He had been regarded as an idiot and employed as a swineherd but now recovered his senses. There follow a number of romantic adventures. Figure 129 shows Berto della Massa of Imola who was a bogus hermit and disgraced his cloth.

There is no real clue as to the identity of the engraver but he might have been John Thompson or one of his apprentices. Thompson appears to have encouraged the use of romantic subjects, as may be gathered from the next piece to be discussed. He allowed his apprentice, Richard Westell, to attend the Academy Schools but with the result that the latter abandoned the engraving of silver and painted romantic subjects for the rest of his life.

4. The Westminster tobacco-box is now deposited on loan at the Westminster City Hall. A full account of it and its cases was published privately by Peter Winckworth in 1966, who had already published an article on 'A unique silver "Box" in a new London home' in *The Connoisseur*, May 1965, pp. 19–20. Although changes in the poor laws have deprived the overseers of all their functions, there still survives the Past Overseers Society to whose clerk, Mr. Gordon P. Child, I am indebted for help.

5. The portrait is adapted from a painting in the National Portrait Gallery by the Jewish artist Frederick Benjamin Barlin, but it looks as if there may have been a miniature in between.

6. I must record my thanks to Miss Margaret Gill who is a specialist on Bewick and who directed my research at the Laing Art Gallery.

7. We get a glimpse of how Bewick arrived at his charges from a loose slip inserted in the account for work executed for Mrs. Anne Robertson (Widow of J. Langland's partner) in 1801. For the engraving of Alderman Cramlington's cup was charged 19s. 6d. which was made up as follows:

Inscription on bottom 241 letters	13s. 4d.
Town motto	2s. 2d.
Arms [of town?]	6d.
Arms [of Cramlington?]	3s. 6d.
	————
	19s. 6d.

8. *Memoirs* (1961 edition), chapter IV, p. 51.

9. Several such commissions are recorded in the account-books, e.g. 'Jan. 1787. A Brig at anchor and an Inscription on a Tankard for Capt. Piercy 10s. 6d.'

10. I am inclined to attribute to Bewick the engraving on a flagon made by Langlands and Robertson in 1783 belonging to West Tanfield Church, near Ripon, showing shields of the arms of Glanvil and Francis suspended from a tree.

11. Edward Dewing was killed as a result of an accident in the hunting-field in 1827. The occasion for the presentation of the waiter was his gift of a pack of hounds (*Norfolk Gazette*, 24 March 1808). I am indebted for these details to a note by Montague Weekley in *Country Life*, 7 March 1968, p. 540.

12. He sometimes received an enquiry as to whether a certain piece was engraved by him or by one of his apprentices (*Bewick to Dovaston, Letters*, ed. Gordon Wilkes, 1968, p. 69).

Chapter VI

1806 to 1900

During the nineteenth century the English goldsmiths' trade had its ups and downs but even when it was prosperous the engravers did not benefit greatly. It was a period during which there was competition between several different styles only some of which allowed much opportunity for engravers. During the Regency period they fared rather poorly. The firm of Rundell, Bridge and Rundell, goldsmiths to the King and to the Prince of Wales, dominated the trade until its dissolution in 1842. The artistic direction was in the hands of John Bridge who was a superb salesman and was able to impose his own taste not only upon his customers but on his rivals. His early training had been as a jeweller so that when he became responsible for the designing of plate, he had to rely upon outside talent. His preference was for monumental pieces in the Roman Imperial style and in recent years it has been possible to identify a number of the first-class artists whom he employed to design and model. For most of his active life—he died in 1834—the actual execution of the work was carried out in the workshops either of Paul Storr or Digby Scott and Benjamin Smith. It is clear that Bridge did not care for engraving on silver but there were occasions when custom demanded its use, such as on the large tea-trays on which his customers expected to see their coats-of-arms. For such work Bridge had to find an engraver who could be relied upon not to discredit his firm.

John Thompson of Gutter Lane appears to have worked up a considerable business at the end of the eighteenth century but died in 1801. His last apprentice was Walter Jackson who has already been mentioned (page 115) and who only became free in the year of his master's death. Bridge had a talent for picking up promising young artists and craftsmen at the beginning of their careers and it would seem that he discovered Jackson at a very early stage, since the latter had already taken on two apprentices within a year of obtaining his own freedom.[1] The patronage of the firm of Rundell, Bridge and Rundell was very valuable but not inspiring, since careful workmanship was all that was expected. The heraldry, whether simple or complicated, is stiff and formal and shows little understanding of the objects depicted. The renderings of the royal

140. WALTER JACKSON
SALVER, gilt, engraved with arms of
George III
1808 hallmark. Mark of Benjamin Smith.
D. 12 in (30·4 cm)
*Victoria and Albert Museum (Wellington
Museum). See page 125*

141. WALTER JACKSON
SALVER, gilt, one of a set of three of
different sizes. Engraved about 1825 with
the arms of the first Marquess of
Ormonde
1809 hallmark. Mark of Benjamin and
James Smith. W. 29½ in (75 cm)
Marquess of Ormonde. See page 125

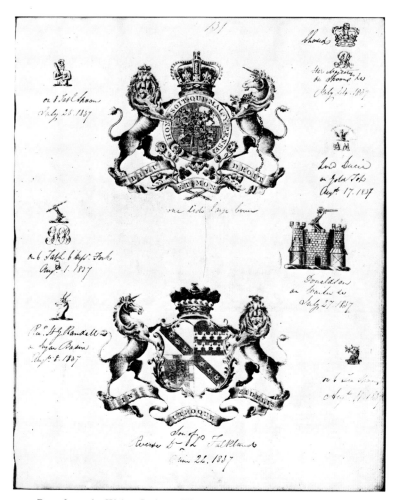

142. Page from the Walter Jackson Album with the arms of William IV and other arms and crests all dated 1837
Victoria and Albert Museum. See page 125

arms are particularly uninspired (Figure 140) whilst those of the Marquess of Ormonde, found on some large trays, showing his arms as an Irish marquess accolé with those as an English baron, are pompously absurd (Figure 141).[2] Walter Jackson became a liveryman of the Goldsmiths' Company in 1824 and died in 1834. In 1815 he had taken as apprentice Samuel Jackson who was perhaps a nephew, who became free in 1822 and who eventually took over the business which he carried on into the third quarter of the century. In 1976 the Victoria and Albert Museum acquired an album of pulls of the crests and arms engraved by the two Jacksons, and the illustration (Figure 142) shows their limitations. Unfortunately their tradition was predominant for the greater part of the reign of Victoria. Too much blame must not be accorded to the

143, 144. W. J. Deere
TWO PLAQUES engraved, respectively, with the arms of the Prince of Wales (later Edward VII), and the 'Art of Printing' (?),
awarded prizes by the Goldsmiths' Company in 1884
Goldsmiths' Company. See page 126

Jacksons since this was a period when the members of the College of Arms, rich in antiquarian lore but not in taste, were issuing heraldic works which passed through numerous editions. The illustrations of arms were copied uncritically by the silver-engravers. Some were better than others and developed a real feeling for heraldry. The low standard of heraldic engraving was symptomatic of the unsatisfactory condition of British industrial art and led to the establishment of a Government School of Design at Somerset House in 1838. Enlightened masters allowed their apprentices to attend, and C. W. Sherborn[3] was amongst the earliest students. A further effort to improve the standard of armorial engraving was made in 1871 when the Goldsmiths' Company started offering annual competitions to improve the designing and execution of work in the precious metals. In 1884 one of the prescribed subjects was an engraving of the arms of the Prince of Wales (Figure 143) and the prize (£20) was awarded to W. J. Deere, who received a similar sum 'for the best specimen of ornamental engraving on silver' (Figure 144).

Whereas John Bridge only allowed the use of engraving in order to satisfy the ancestral pride of his customers and did not regard sufficiently critically the work of the Jacksons, a few other goldsmiths were rather more venturesome. In the later years of the Regency there arose a demand for plate made in the style of earlier periods other than the late Roman. The Anglo–Dutch fashion of the Charles II period was imitated, particularly for ornamental sideboard dishes. These had richly embossed rims whilst the centres might be set with embossed plaques (sometimes of an earlier date). A pair of gilt dishes (Figure 145) made in 1824 by Edward Farrell, whose designs tended to be unusual, has the centre engraved with the arms of Sir Henry Fetherstonehaugh Bart., of Uppark, Sussex, with a surround copied from a design by Stefano della Bella (1610–64).

Within a few years of the death of John Bridge in 1834, there began to appear a fresh variety of plate which was still in the classical style but elaborately engraved. It is not clear who originated it or why its appearance was so long delayed. English connoisseurs had been collecting 'Etruscan vases' for many years and catalogues illustrated with engravings had long been available. The forms of the pieces were either copied or adapted from those of Greek vases, but the engraved decoration is still in the opulent style of the Roman Imperial period which Bridge had always favoured. A ewer bearing the mark of Reily and Storer with the 1840 hallmark is a good early example (Figure 146). The Etruscan style was never the monopoly of one firm but Barnards were using it freely a few years later. On 17 January 1848 they booked an order from J. Meyer, Liverpool, for 'an Etruscan Tea Kettle Eng^d subjects Pandora & Golden Age pick^d ground as before £95'. On 19 February they supplied Widdowson and Veale 'a $3\frac{1}{4}$ quart

145. SIDEBOARD DISH, gilt. Engraved with the arms of Sir Henry Fetherstonehaugh, Bart., within a cartouche after Stefano della Bella (d. 1664)
1824 hallmark. Mark of Edward Farrell. D. 15 in (38·5 cm)
Messrs. Christie. See page 127

146. EWER, engraved with figures of Apollo, Diana and Pan, against an engraved (not pickled) ground
1840 hallmark. Mark of Reily and Storer. H. 12½ in (31·5 cm)
Messrs. Thomas Lumley. See page 127

147. HOT-WATER JUG engraved after the Portland Vase
1871 hallmark. Mark of W. G. Sissons. H. 9 in (23 cm)
Messrs. Thomas Lumley. See page 129

148. VASE, gilt, the central band with pickled (acid-bitten) ground
1864 Sheffield hallmark. Mark of Roberts and Belk. H. 14½ in (37 cm)
Messrs. Thomas Lumley. See page 129

ovolo edge Etruscan Tea Kettle engraved by them, subjects by Flaxman & ground pick^d by us'. Barnards did not only supply 'Etruscan Tea Kettles' but also jugs and vases. On 12 July 1861, they booked an order from H. H. Dobson for 'a 3 Pint Etruscan vase w^h cover [Queen's Guernsey Race Cup, 1862], engraved Etruscan orn. by Donald, The House & Horses of the Sun on the other [side]'. These quotations emphasize the complicated relationships of the silversmithing trade in Victorian times.[4] Flaxman had died in 1826 and is not known to have engraved silver. The Victorian engravers may have got hold of drawings of plate which he had designed for Rundell, Bridge and Rundell, or else his name had become attached to his style. Next it will be noted that subjects engraved by one firm might have pickled (acid-bitten) grounds added by another. Although Barnards maintained an engraving workshop they are found passing out work to Donald, and similarly Widdowson and Veale had their engraver, but the task of adding the pickled background was left to Barnards. This was very much a family firm and when its mark was entered in 1829 it incorporated the initials of Edward Barnard, Edward Barnard junior, John Barnard and William Barnard. It would seem that William[5] was in charge of the engraving, though in order to take advantage of freedom by patrimony his nephew James Faraday was apprenticed in 1858 to his father John to learn engraving, and his grandson Archie Evelyn Barnard was bound in 1883 specifically to learn heraldic engraving. Members of the family could not meet all the engraving needs of the firm and James Faraday Barnard is credited with nine apprentices, nearly all of whom completed their terms. This must not be taken to imply that Barnards was particularly noted for its heraldic work but merely that being a large firm, it was necessary to employ a number of engravers capable of marking spoons, forks, etc.

The popularity of the 'Etruscan' style lasted almost until the end of the century and in London the firm of W. G. Sissons used it extensively during the seventies. A hot-water jug of 1871 has its body engraved with subjects derived from the Portland Vase (Figure 147). A complete tea and coffee set produced in the following year is less successful although meticulously engraved with classical ornament derived from some architectural handbook. The same defect is seen on the plate decorated in this style by the Sheffield firm of Roberts and Belk who sometimes marred a quite good classical form by too lavish decoration, as on a vase bearing the 1864 hallmark (Figure 148). This firm also sold electrotype tea and coffee sets decorated in the same style.

Plate engraved with historical and genre subjects was not common in the nineteenth century. The most important series is to be found on the various cases made for the tobacco-box belonging to the Overseers of the Poor of the Parishes of St. Margaret and St. John, Westminster. The case made for the years 1809 to 1826 has on the lid an inscription recording the amount collected and distributed to the poor in commemoration of the fiftieth anniversary of the accession of George III in 1809. Around the cover are oblong plaques representing the battle of Waterloo (*J. Swaine sc.*),

149. Detail of a WAITER engraved with 'The Exeter Mail' in 1821
1762 hallmark
Royal Albert Museum, Exeter. See page 130

whilst around the sides are upright plaques commemorating the acquittal of Queen Caroline and the death of Princess Charlotte etc. All the plaques are engraved by book-illustrators of average capacity but the standard is higher than that of the plaques used later in the century. Some of these last have no pictures but merely an inscription recording the events of the year in various scripts as on a tombstone.

The trend in designs for testimonials was generally unfavourable for the engravers. There was no adequate successor for engraving genre subjects after the death of Bewick in 1828 and the waiter engraved in 1821 for presentation to the driver of the Exeter Mail (Figure 149) is feeble by comparison. When the engravers strayed away from folk art the results might be deplorable as may be gathered from the description of one of the pieces shown at the Great Exhibition of 1851 which runs as follows: 'Tea-tray illustrative of the purposes of the Exhibition. The ship of all nations commanded by Britannia and steered by Father Thames . . . engraved medallions in border showing trading between nations, steam navigation and machinery. Engraved and designed by Donald and Son.' (Exhibited by Angell, George, 51 Compton Street, Clerkenwell.)[6] Probably Donald and Son decorated also the tea-trays engraved with newly built civic buildings which are now to be found in the strongrooms of town halls. Major testimonials continued to be made in the monumental style which had been favoured by John Bridge but which usually only allowed a limited scope for the engravers. In 1880 Hunt and Roskell were commissioned by the Nottingham Water Company to make a testimonial for presentation to Thomas Hawksley who had gained a reputation as a

150. SALVER belonging to
the Hawksley centrepiece
1880 hallmark. Mark of
Hunt and Roskell
Victoria and Albert Museum.
See page 132

151. Detail of the
HAWKSLEY SALVER,
showing the Italian Garden
in Kensington Gardens

152. The Japanese Taste
a. TRAY, gilt. 1878 hallmark. Mark of W. and J. Barnard. W. 9¾ in (25 cm)
b. CHRISTENING-MUG. 1874 hallmark. Mark of Anne Millson
c. TEAPOT, parcel-gilt. 1896 Sheffield hallmark. Mark of Mappin and Webb
d. FISH-SERVERS. 1888 Sheffield hallmark. Mark of J. N. Mappin
Messrs. Thomas Lumley. See page 133

designer of reservoirs, pumping-stations etc. It is designed as a monumental fountain surmounted by a nymph emptying a pitcher of water, and stands upon a round salver engraved with six of the works designed by Hawksley (Figure 150). As may be seen from the view of the Italian Garden in Kensington Gardens (Figure 151) the scenes are only up to the standard of those appearing in the *Illustrated London News*.

The fashion for Japanese art began to influence English silver in the seventies. In 1877 the Mikado commissioned from Hunt and Roskell a service of plate to be made with Western forms but Japanese ornament. Judging from the illustration in the *Art Journal*[7] the result was appalling but since the decoration was not engraved, it does not concern us. Although Hunt and Roskell had been alerted to Japanese art, they do not

153. FREDERICK ELKINGTON, designer
TEA-SET, gilt. 1879 hallmark. Mark of Elkington and Co. Tray 14 in (36 cm) across, Teapot H. 3 in
(7·5 cm)
Messrs. Thomas Lumley. See page 133

seem to have realized its adaptability to engraving. When the object to be decorated
could not be given a Japanese look, as in the case of a christening-mug or fish-servers
(Figure 152), only the ornament came from the Far East. Considerable ingenuity was
used in borrowing the forms of articles in common use in Japan and adapting them for
English use. The leading firm was Elkington of Birmingham,[8] and the design for the
tea-trays (Figure 153) was registered by Frederick Elkington on 27 March 1880. Two
versions are known, both inspired by Japanese painted fans and decorated with birds
amongst blossoms and bamboos. One has a rim simulating bamboo but the other has a
handle which must have been impractical when the tray was loaded with teapot, milk-
jug, and sugar-bowl, all made *en suite*. The fashion for plate in the Japanese style lasted
from 1870 to 1900, and rather more firms used it than had worked in the engraved
'Etruscan' style.

133

154. WILLIAM BUTTERFIELD, designer
FLAGON, gilt and set with carbuncles
1844 hallmark. Mark of I. J. Keith. H. 15½ in (39 cm)
Christ Church, Albany Street. See page 135

155. A. W. N. PUGIN, designer
FLAGON, parcel-gilt
1844 Birmingham hallmark. Mark of Hardman and Iliffe. H. 10½
in (26·5 cm)
St. Thomas's Church, Elson, Gosport, Hampshire. See page 135

It might be expected that the encouragement given to the church arts by the
Tractarians would have resulted in the production of much plate decorated with
engraving. In actual fact this only happened at the lowest level. William Butterfield
published, under the patronage of the Oxford Architectural Society and the
Cambridge Camden Society, volumes illustrating English medieval plate with the
intention that they should be adapted or copied. This was done extensively by the

134

chosen firm, I. J. Keith, and chalices were produced engraved with one of the customary inscriptions round the bowl, and a device on the foot and on the middle of the paten. Butterfield's plates are insensitive so that it is not surprising that the engravers employed by I. J. Keith produced only mediocre results. Occasionally Butterfield might introduce some engraving as on the flagon (adapted from a medieval cruet) belonging to Christ Church, Albany Street (Figure 154). This was executed by I. J. Keith in 1844 and has an inscribed band round the middle and rather weak floral scrolls above and below.

In the same year Hardman and Iliffe of Birmingham made for Archdeacon Wilberforce[9] a flagon for the new church at Elson, near Gosport. It is shaped like a tankard (Figure 155) with a conventional black-letter inscription round the top whilst the body is decorated with a spiral vine-scroll. Although A. W. N. Pugin was closely connected with Hardmans, it is difficult to attribute to him so weak a design. Most of the other Victorian designers of church plate did not allow much scope for the engravers and when attempting to give a rich effect would rely on other techniques or materials. Enamel, filigree and semi-precious stones were all used.

The exception was William Burges who was a much more serious antiquary than Butterfield or Pugin. He spent some time in the office of Sir Matthew Digby Wyatt and contributed some of the drawings for the latter's *Metalwork* (1852). He realized the need for analysing the merits and defects of the various goldsmithing techniques which he summarized in an article in 1858 in the *Ecclesiologist*.[10] His section on engraving reads as follows:

> Now engraving hardly tells of itself, unless the lines are exceedingly bold, and filled up with either with niello or enamel,[11] or some other substance. It is also advisable that the figures should be well detached from the ground by cross hatching, and not by only one series of lines going one way, as is too often the case. When there is no ground the engraving consists merely of an outline, it is well to keep the lines firm to the very end, and simply turn them off bluntly, as we see on monumental brasses, and not to end them by gradually decreasing their force.

Burges did not show a marked preference for engraving but when he designed for it he left little chance for the engraver to go wrong, as may be seen from the meticulous pen-and-ink drawings preserved in an album entitled *Orfèvrerie ecclesiastical* in the library of the Royal Institute of British Architects. He took trouble to discover the good engravers and did not hand out his work to one firm.[12] This resulted in the production of pieces in the style of the chosen period but not mere fakes. His most important engraved pieces were hallmarked between 1861–4 and bear witness not only to his understanding of medieval art but also of its iconography.[13] The earliest is a chalice and paten for the church of Holme-on-Spalding-Moor, near Market Weighton. The engraving on the foot of the chalice is arranged in two tiers and engraved with representations of Christ

156. WILLIAM BURGES, designer
CHALICE, formerly parcel-gilt
1862 hallmark. Mark of Charles Hart and Son. H. 7¾ (19·5 cm)
Selsley Church, Gloucestershire. See page 137

157. WILLIAM BURGES, designer
FLAGON
1862 hallmark. Mark of Charles Hart and Son. H. 7¾
in (19·5 cm)
Selsley Church, Gloucestershire. See page 137

158. WILLIAM BURGES, designer
CHALICE, parcel-gilt and set with semi-precious stones
1862 Birmingham hallmark. Mark of John Hardman and Co. H. 6¾ in
(17 cm)
St. Michael and All Angels Church, Brighton. See page 139

the King, Christ the Sacrifice, and the Four Evangelists and their symbols. An inscription shows that it was ready in 1862. He was evidently not satisfied with it since a repeat of the same design for All Saints, Selsley, Gloucestershire, was made by Hart and Son, and is hallmarked 1862 (Figure 156). For Selsley the same firm executed in the same year a flagon having a bulbous body engraved with roundels enclosing half-figures of David, Melchisedisec, Abel and Noah (Figure 157). Both chalice and flagon carry appropriate inscriptions in well-designed gothic lettering. There is no reason for thinking that Burges was dissatisfied with the work of Hart's engraver, so it is difficult to explain why his most important work bears the mark of John Hardman and Co. with the

159. Drawings by WILLIAM BURGES for the engraving on the chalice shown as Figure 158. Some of the guardians of the gates of 'The Heavenly Jerusalem', and the 'River Phison'.
Royal Institute of British Architects. See page 139

Birmingham hallmark for 1862. It is a chalice made for St. Michael and All Angels, Brighton (Figure 158). It is an elaborate essay in early fourteenth-century art, more especially that of the Rhine and Meuse. The round foot is engraved with 'The Four Rivers of Paradise', 'The Tree of Life' and 'The Tree of Knowledge' and 'The Heavenly Jerusalem' with its twelve gates guarded by angels. In the album of *Orfèvrerie ecclesiastical* are the drawings for both the Selsley and the Brighton chalice (Figure 159) which demonstrate the care taken by Burges in directing the engravers. A flagon similar to that made for Selsley was made for St. Michael and All Angels in 1862 by Hart and Son who executed for the same church another chalice bearing the 1864 hallmark and having the foot engraved with half-figures of Christ in the act of blessing, and the Archangels Michael, Gabriel and Raphael. Burges continued to design church plate but relied on other techniques, especially enamel, for illustrating the symbolism to which he was so much attached.[14]

During the seventeenth and eighteenth centuries important churches had a large silver alms-dish which was placed between the two candlesticks on the communion-table. Although generally engraved only with an 'I H S', occasionally they might carry a figure subject, as at Dunham Massey (Figure 90) and St. Lawrence Jewry (Figure 119). There are no important alms-dishes engraved in Victorian times. The Tractarians favoured placing a cross between the candlesticks. Alms-dishes shrank in size and importance, since they were now placed on the credence table. The other changes brought about by the Tractarians did not create fresh work for the engravers and it became rare for the arms of a donor to be engraved on the plate which he had presented.

In the period covered by this work it might appear that the art of engraving on silver had moved in a circle. This is in fact a fallacy since a circle consists of a continuous line whereas we have been concerned with one in which there are gaps. During the Middle Ages there was a limited number of skilled engravers as well as a much larger number of less proficient. The introduction of printing led to the appearance of a number of engravers who were equally competent to work on silver or copper. This lasted from the middle of the sixteenth until the middle of the eighteenth century. After that date the association became weaker, and ultimately the printers became much less dependent upon the engravers as a result of the introduction of new techniques for illustrations. With the growth of art schools and technical colleges, aspiring students ceased to apprentice themselves to engravers of silver in order to obtain a basic training in design. It is not therefore surprising that artists who could both design and execute engraving on silver became rare and this deficiency was hardly affected by the growth of designers, like William Burges, who could design but not engrave. The mid-nineteenth-century tendency to overload plate with ornament (not necessarily engraved) ultimately led to a reaction to simplicity which eliminated engraving. The demand for heraldic engraving was still strong in 1900, though the efforts which were being made to improve the standard had not yet had much success. The long-standing separation of the crafts of making and of engraving plate nowadays operates against the engravers, since the designers generally cater for pure silversmithing. This is, of course, the opposite to the conditions under which Gribelin, Simpson etc. had worked in the eighteenth century when the distinction of a piece of plate often derived from its engraving. It is surely time for the engravers to be given greater opportunities to demonstrate their skill.

Notes

1. It is possible that Bridge may merely have transferred his custom from the recently deceased John Thompson to whom Jackson had been bound.

2. In 1811 the eighteenth Earl of Ormonde recovered from the British Treasury a payment of £216,000 for arrears of payments on the prisage of wines imported into Ireland, granted by Edward I to his ancestor. He immediately started on a spending spree, making large purchases from Rundell, Bridge and Rundell. The arms on the trays are those of his brother who succeeded him and who was created marquess in 1825, having been made a K.P. in 1821. Clearly the trays must all have been re-engraved.

3. I have been unable to trace any examples of the work of Charles William Sherborn done during his apprenticeship (1845–52) to Robert Oliver of Rupert Street, although his son mentions in his memoir that he had tracings signed by his father. It is not clear how much plate he engraved during the years 1856–72 when he was working for the trade. In 1856 he exhibited at the Royal Academy an Indian ink drawing roundel of the arms of the Prince of Wales. After 1872 he confined himself to the production of a superb series of heraldic book-plates.

4. I am indebted for these references from the Barnard ledgers to Mrs. Shirley Bury.

5. At Goldsmiths' Hall he was only described as a plate-worker.

6. *Catalogue of the Great Exhibition*, Vol. II, class 23. Donald, W. J. and C., appears also in Vol. I.

7. 1877, p. 45.

8. The firm had branches in Liverpool and London. Some of its work was hallmarked at Goldsmiths' Hall instead of at Birmingham.

9. Later Bishop of Oxford and known as 'Soapy Sam'.

10. XIX, 1858, p. 222.

11. Most Victorians did not differentiate between niello and enamel. Burges sometimes had inscriptions filled in with black enamel (Figures 156 and 158) but did not usually have the engraving filled in (as may be seen from the illustrations). He may have changed his mind on this subject.

12. In 1864 he replaced Street as supervisor of the scheme of the Ecclesiological Society for the manufacture of plate and transferred its patronage from I. J. Keith to Jes Barkentin. Probably he had not been satisfied by Keith's execution of his chalice, hallmarked 1861, for Holme-on-Spalding-Moor, Humberside.

13. He was in touch with the great French antiquary, Didron.

14. It is likely that more repeats of the engraved work of the early sixties will come to light.

Appendix I

Catalogue of the Works Attributed to the Engraver *P over M*

The pieces here listed share certain peculiarities. It was not the universal practice abroad for engravers to sign their work and signatures are found more commonly on prints than on plate. There is, therefore, no special significance in the presence or absence of a signature. The Buccleuch plates (No. 4), the bowls at the Victoria and Albert Museum (No. 5), and the ewer and basin (No. 6) are unsigned, and in some of the other sets only some are signed. The scene of Joshua's fight against the Amalek in the centre of the basin (No. 3) is signed twice. The identification of the Old Testament subjects is in most cases by the chapter references in Genesis and Exodus.

1. SET OF TWELVE PLATES silver-gilt (Figure 30). Engraved with Old Testament subjects.
   Signed. No contemporary hallmark.† No goldsmith's mark.
   Diameter $7\frac{3}{4}$ in (20 cm).

Rims engraved with two panels filled with Latin captions. The scenes depicted in the centres are mostly adapted from the *Quadrins Historique de la Bible* of Bernard Salomon, 1553 (or else from some earlier series). The rims are also engraved with profile heads in roundels and sporting scenes. The scene in the centre of each plate is framed in a laurel wreath with the number of the subject depicted below. The scenes marked with * are not related to the *Quadrins Historique*.

(1) Abram's journey through Canaan to Egypt.
(2) Abram refreshed by Melchisedek.*
(3) Destruction of Sodom and Gomorrah.
(4) Sacrifice of Isaac.
(5) Rebecca at the well.

† All the plates are marked with the Strasbourg mark with 13. This version of the mark was only introduced at the end of the seventeenth century (Jacques Helft, *Le poinçon des Provinces Françaises*, 1968, p. 374), but according to the authorities of the Strasbourg Museum its use was made compulsory in 1639.

(6) Birth of Esau and Jacob.

(7) Jacob steals Esau's birthright.*

(8) Jacob's ladder.

(9) Jacob rescued by Reuben from the well.*

(10) Potiphar's wife.

(11) Joseph expounds Pharaoh's dream (Figure 30).

(12) Joseph recognizes his brethren.

2. SET OF TWELVE PLATES parcel-gilt (Figure 32). Engraved with simplified versions of a series of prints dated 1550 by Heinrich Aldegraver.

Three signed. Hallmark for 1567 (the date-letter K is that used by Richard Rogers who was dismissed on Christmas Eve 1567). Goldsmith's mark *hooded falcon* (Thomas Bampton).

Diameter $7\frac{3}{4}$ in (20 cm).

Rims engraved with four roundels with profile heads separated by panels filled with floral scrolls. Centres each filled with one of 'The Labours of Hercules'. They are arranged here in the order illustrated in Figure 32.

(1) Kills centaur and releases Hippodamia.

(2) Strangles two serpents whilst in his cradle (*signed*).

(3) Fights with Achelous over Deianira.

(4) Wrestles with Antaeus.

(5) Erects the Pillars of Hercules (*signed*).

(6) Kills Cacus with his club.

(7) Beats the Lernean Hydra.

(8) Kills the Nemean lion (*signed*).

(9) Captures the Arcadian stag.

(10) Drags Cerberus from Hades.

(11) Rescues Deianira from Nessus.

(12) Kills the dragon guarding the Garden of the Hesperides.

When sold as Lot 467 at the Parke Bernet Galleries, New York, on 1 November 1947, as part of the collection of J. Pierpont Morgan, their history was given as follows:

Collection of Sir Robert Bruce Cotton (1571–1631), the antiquary, Founder of the Cottonian Library, in whose family they descended until 1757.

Collection of Mary Cotton (m. 1757) of Connington, Huntingdon, wife of Basil, 6th Earl of Denbigh.

Collection of Rudolph William, 8th Earl of Denbigh.

Crichton Bros. Ltd., London.

On the back of each plate are traces of an inscription and of a coat-of-arms surmounted by a mitre. They do not look to be contemporary.

Appendix I

Whilst there seems to be a tradition that these plates came to the earls of Denbigh from the Cottons, it does not seem possible to substantiate this by documents. Sir Robert Bruce Cotton was not born at the time these plates were hallmarked and his father was a person of only local importance.

The plates are now the property of the Southern Comfort Corporation.

3. EWER AND BASIN, parcel-gilt (Figures 33-5).
   Signed and dated 1567. Hallmark for 1567 (the date-letter is the K used by Thomas Keelynge who succeeded Richard Rogers after Christmas 1567). Goldsmith's mark *L reversed* (Jackson, p. 101).
   Ewer, Height 13¼ in (34 cm); Basin, Diameter 19½ in (50 cm).

Ewer, the egg-shaped body engraved with full-length representations of William I, William II, Henry I, Stephen and Henry II under an arcade of laurel and with their names and titles. Above are roundels with half-length representations of John, Henry III, Edward I, Edward II and Edward III.

Basin, with central boss engraved with a battle scene which is identified by 'EXO 17' which relates to Joshua's fight with Amalek, whilst Moses with sagging arms, is seated in the background. The scene is signed twice, once with also the date 1567. This proves that the engraving must have been executed between Christmas 1567 when Keelynge's date-letter came into use, and 24 March 1568 which was the end of the year 1567 according to the reckoning then used. Around the boss is inscribed the not obviously appropriate inscription adapted from I john 5:7: SANGVIS IESV CHRISTI FILY DEI EMVNDAT NOS AB ONMI PECCATO IOHANNIS I CV' ('The blood of Our Lord Jesus Christ the Son of God cleanseth us from all sin'). Surrounding the central boss are half-length portraits of Henry VIII, Edward VI, Mary I and Elizabeth I, separated by four Old Testament scenes (Jacob and Rachel at the well, the Sacrifice of Isaac, Abram's journey through Canaan into Egypt, and Lot entertaining two angels). Rim engraved with roundels with representations of Edward II (should be Richard II), Henry IV, Henry V, Henry VI, Edward IV, Edward V, Richard III and Henry VII separated by Old Testament subjects (Aaron's rod turned into a serpent, the Passover, Birth of Esau and Jacob, Joseph rescued by Reuben from the well, Joseph and Potiphar's wife, Joseph expounds Pharaoh's dream).

The Old Testament scenes are adapted from the woodcuts in the *Quadrins Historique de la Bible* (or else some earlier version) but the source of the representations of the English sovereigns has not been traced.

Acquired by J. Pierpont Morgan from Crichton Bros., with the information that they had been heirlooms of the Hyde family. At the sale of the Morgan silver, they were acquired by C. Ruxton Love who eventually gave them to the Metropolitan Museum of Art, New York.

4. SET OF TWELVE PLATES, parcel-gilt (Figures 36–7 and Frontispiece).
Engraved with the parable of 'The Prodigal Son'.
No signatures. Hallmark for 1568 (one 1569). Goldsmith's mark
FR in monogram (Jackson, p. 100).
Diameter $7\frac{1}{2}$ in (19 cm).

Rims engraved with three ovals filled either with profile heads or else with birds, separated by panels with stems laden with fruit or flowers.
In the middle are the following scenes:
 (1) The Prodigal Son leaves his father's house.
 (2) Goes into a far country (Frontispiece).
 (3) Kisses a woman outside an inn.
 (4) Feasting.
 (5) Wenching.
 (6) Raping.
 (7) Turned away by a harlot.
 (8) Discards his gaming utensils and musical instruments.
 (9) Employed as a swineherd.
 (10) Repents.
 (11) Received back by his father.
 (12) Feasted on the fatted calf.

These are not ancient possessions of the dukes of Buccleuch since E. Alfred Jones (*Old Furniture*, VII, 1929, pp. 93–9) records that they were acquired at the Strawberry Hill sale in 1842 and had previously belonged to the great Earl of Clarendon from whose descendant Horace Walpole had acquired them. It will have been noted that the ewer and basin (No. 3) are also stated to have belonged to the Hyde family, but Lord Chancellor Clarendon's fortunes needed to be rebuilt at the Restoration and, as far as is known, none of his ancestors could have afforded very expensive plate in Elizabethan times.

5. SET OF SIX BOWLS, silver-gilt (Figures 38–9). Engraved with Old Testament subjects and ocean scenes.
No signatures. Hallmark for 1573. Goldsmith's mark *FR in monogram* (Jackson, p. 100).
Diameter 10 in (25.5 cm).

Rims engraved with panels containing floral scrolls with animals, two roundels with birds and an escutcheon with a pounced coat-of-arms. Round the central depression are sea-monsters, mermen and in the middle the following scenes:
 (1) Abram and Sarai praying for a son.

(2) Abram entertaining three angels.

(3) Sacrifice of Isaac (Figure 38).

(4) Rebecca at the well.

(5) Meeting of Isaac and Rebecca (Figure 39).

(6) Jacob steals the blessing of Isaac.

These engravings are not related to the Old Testament subjects on the set of plates (No. 1) or on the basin (No. 3). They must derive from some other series of woodcuts by a less skilful artist than Bernard Salomon. The maritime scenes are somewhat reminiscent of those of Adriaen Collaert of Antwerp but there is considerable doubt about the date of his birth which is given by Thieme-Becker as about 1560 but by Linnig (*La Gravure en Belgique*, 1911) as about 1545. It would be unwise to press this attribution since the cartographers were prone to fill in the empty spaces in their maps with sea-monsters etc. The decoration of the rims are very much in the style of Vergil Solis (1514-62).

This is the latest of this group to come to light, since its existence was unknown until it was offered for sale by Christie's on 3 July 1946, and was speedily acquired for the Victoria and Albert Museum from Thomas Lumley. The escutcheon pounced on the rim of each bowl is that of Montagu with the difference for a fifth son. This points to William, fifth son of Sir Edward Montagu, Lord Chief Justice (d. 1556). William is a shadowy figure who spent most of his life at Oakley, Bedfordshire, where the church holds his monument with epitaph stating 'he lived 73 years a Bachelor and soe died on 28th September, 1691.' His will does not seem to have survived but his executor was his neighbour and nephew Edward, later created Lord Montagu of Boughton. The bowls seem to have remained with the Montagu family, since when they were sold it was by Captain Frederick Montagu who could trace his descent from the first Lord Montagu of Boughton.

6. EWER AND BASIN, parcel-gilt (Figures 40-2). Engraved with Old Testament subjects and with the arms of Pallandt and van Dorth accolé.
   Unsigned. Goldsmith's mark *BI in an oval*. Dated 1575.
   Ewer, Height 16 in (41 cm); Basin, Diameter 18 in (46 cm).

Ewer, the egg-shaped body engraved with four scenes from the story of Joseph:

(1) He is taken out of the well.

(2) Potiphar's wife.

(3) He is sold to the Ishmaelites.

(4) He expounds Pharaoh's dream.

Basin, with central boss engraved with the arms and date. The depression and the rim are both engraved with a girdle design consisting of alternate oval links engraved with

scenes from the story of Abram and roundels engraved with profile heads of the Twelve
Caesars. Background etched with arabesques. The scenes round the central depression
are:

(5) Abram's journey through Canaan to Egypt.
(6) Disagreement between the herdsmen of Abram and Lot.
(7) Separation of Abram and Lot.
(8) Abram is refreshed by Melchisedek.

Round the rim are:

(9) Abram's vision in which Canaan is promised.
(10) Hagar is sent back by an angel to Sarai (Figure 42).
(11) Abram renews his covenant with the Lord and entertains three messengers.
(12) Abram warned of the destruction of Sodom.
(13) Lot with his two daughters in a cave.
(14) Abram makes a feast; Hagar and Ishmael cast out.
(15) Hagar and Ishmael comforted by an angel.
(16) Sacrifice of Isaac.

The place where the goldsmith *BI* worked has not been identified. The Pallandt family
was domiciled in the Protestant duchy of Cleves. The four scenes on the ewer are based
on engravings by Vergil Solis dated 1520, whilst those on the basin are adapted from the
same cycle of Old Testament scenes by Bernard Salomon that are used on Nos. 1 and 3.

Carl Meyer de Rothschild Collection, Galerie George Petit, Paris, 12–13 June 1911,
Lot 11.
Kurt Meyer of Los Angeles, Christie's, 27 March 1974, Lot 71.
Believed to be in Germany.

Appendix II

Apprenticeships of Engravers

The search for the engravers of silver is only beginning but the following hints may be of use to those who engage in it. The first suggestion is to trace the professional ancestry of identified engravers since an apprentice was bound to his master for the purpose of learning his art. It can, therefore, be assumed usually that the master was competent to engrave silver. The following is taken from the records of the Goldsmiths' Company.

Apprentice	Bound	Master	Free
David Venables	1660	Father (John)	1668
Benjamin Rhodes	1670	David Venables	1678
William Starling II	1688	Benjamin Rhodes	1698
Charles Gardner	1705	William Starling II	1714
Butler Clowes	1744	Charles Gardner	1755
James Bolton	1766	Butler Clowes	1773

At present it is only possible to attribute work to Rhodes and Gardner.

The following is taken from the records of the Merchant Taylors' Company:

Apprentice	Bound	Master	Free
William Trevethan	1638	Robert Vaughan	1653
Richard Hopthrow	1682	William Trevethan	1698
Ellis Gamble	1702	Richard Hopthrow	1702
William Hogarth	1713	Ellis Gamble	?

At present it is only possible to attribute conjecturally work to Gamble and Hogarth.

Prosperous engravers took on a succession of apprentices, so that although this line of approach is productive, it can be carried on *ad infinitum*. The earlier records of the Goldsmiths' Company give no indication as to apprentices who aimed only at learning specialized skills. Towards the middle of the eighteenth century some apprentices began to be recorded as being bound 'to learn engraving'. Their names and those of their masters are of interest to us. On the other hand, some apprentices who certainly became engravers did not record any limited ambition. This was often the case when one member undertook the engraving for a family firm as, for instance, Walter Angel and James Faraday Barnard. In the following list the names of apprentices who did not take up their freedom have been eliminated. Others, like Richard Westell, R.A., never engraved silver after they had become free. Many apprentices could not afford to take up their freedom and worked as journeymen in the workshops of the more prosperous engravers. The following is a list of those apprentices bound 'to learn engraving' who became free of the Goldsmiths' Company. Only about half of the 450 who had been bound to 'learn engraving' took up their freedom on the completion of their apprenticeships. Impecunious apprentices might not be able to afford to do this until several years after they had served their time.

Apprentice	Bound	Master	Free
Adolpho, Francis R.	1791	James Williamson	1812
Alexander, Thomas J.	1841	Samuel Jackson	1858
Arnold, Thomas J.	1825	William W. Burch	1832
Arrowsmith, Joseph	1803	Joseph Beckwith	1810
Baker, Edward W.	1831	John Ellis	1838
Barnard, Archie E.[1]	1883	Father (James Faraday)	1893
Barnard, Hugh Faraday[1]	1879	Father (James Faraday)	1887
Barnard, James Faraday	. . .[2]	Father (John)	1858
Barnes, William	1810	Vincent Philips	1828
Barnett, James	1760	William Wright	1768
Bawtree, John S.	1791	Father	1804
Bawtree, William	1787	Father	1800
Bell, Thomas F.	1818	John Russell	1826
Bindorff, Daniel	1843	Samuel Hyne	1855
Blake, William	1790	James Williamson	1797
Bolton, James	1766	Butler Clowes	1773
Bowden, Nathaniel	1836	S. Everingham	1843
Bridge, James M.	1853	James P. Gibson	1862
Brunt, Robert P.	1846	John Rumley	1873
Bull, John	1812	William J. White	1820
Bullock, John	1784	John Thompson	1791
Butler, Edward	1786	John Gale	1793
Cannon, Henry	1851	Walter Angell	1858
Cary, John	1770	William Palmer	1778
Childs, John W.	1874	John Faraday Barnard	1881
Cooper, Henry	1797	John Warner	1804

Appendix II

Apprentice	Bound	Master	Free
Couldon, Samuel	1819	W. N. Hughes	1826
Coules, Alfred	1829	C. W. Dix	1859
Cowie, John	1807	W. Sandbed	1814
Culmore, Charles	1798	Edward Edwardes	1806
Dare (Deare), John	1790	J. Whittingham	1803
Davies, James	1793	James Bawtree	1799
Davies, Thomas G.	1799	T. W. Harper	1806
Davis, William T.	1791	John Russell	1796
Debaufer, James	1812	Alex. Findlay	1820
Dighton, Robert	1766	Ben. Godfrey	1773
Dipple, Thomas	. . . .[2]	Father	1827
Dix, James C.	. . . .[2]	Father	1844
Dixon, John T.	1793	John Thompson	1801
Douglas, W. M.	1783	William Morris	1791
Edwards, Edward	1797	William Norris	1811
Ellis, John	1810	Alex. Walkenshaw	1818
Elven, John P.	1776	John Fielding	1795
Embleton, Thomas	1792	George Wilson	1799
Emes, John	1778	William Woollett	1780
Esterbrooke, John	1831	Charles Mullis	1839
Everett, Jones	1789	George Bude	1797
Everingham, Samuel	1817	William Moody	1824
Eves, James	1786	John Warner	1794
Fielder, Robert	1779	John Gale	1787
Fife, George	1772	John Gale	1787
Findlay, Alexander	1803	John Russell	1811
Findlay, Matthew	. . . .[2]	Samuel Everingham	1832
Fisher, William	1823	Charles Mullens	1830
Ford, Thomas	1852	Walter Angell	1862
Foskett, James	1846	John Rumley	1854
Fry, Benjamin	1778	Ann Orpen	1785
Fulcher, George R.	1817	William Hall	1825
Gale, Edward	1776	J. Perkins	1802
Gallagher, Edward A.	1877	G. F. Lacy	1884
Galloway, Robert	1767	John Fielding	1774
Galton, Frank W.	1882	James Faraday Barnard	1890
Gardner, Joseph W.	1852	William Robinson	1860
Gavey, Robert	1790	William Norris	1798
Gay, John L.	1825	Edward Butler	1832

Apprentice	Bound	Master	Free
Gilbert, John	1846	Robert Oliver	1859
Gilson, James P.	1830	George Mills	1838
Glenn, John	1783	John Warner	1790
Graham, Edmund	1781	George Bude	1789
Gretton, Henry	1771	Father	1785
Hall, Joseph W.	1863	Walter Angell	1871
Hall, William	1789	John Whittingham	1797
Harris, William	1806	John Warner	1814
Hartley, George	1851	W. B. Dowsett	1868
Harvey, George	1864	W. A. Shepherd	1872
Hawksworth, John	1802	Henry Woodward	1809
Hazard, John	1826	{ John Tidcombe C. W. Dix	1834
Hearn, Joseph	1793	Edward Edwardes	1802
Hearse, Charles	1860	Father	1868
Hearse, William	1788	John Thompson	1796
Heath, Charles A.	1792	John Gale	1799
Hennell, Robert III	1778	Father (John)	1785
Hill, James C.	1762	George Cobbould	1774
Holden, Edward J. T.	1820	Thomas Dowling	1828
Holloway, Stephen	1800	John Warner	1807
Hollyock, William C.	1845	C. W. Dix	1852
Holyland, John	1808	Thomas Mayfield	1816
Hooker, John	1806	Walter Jackson	1824
Hopkins, Edward	1789	Robert Hennell III	1796
Huffam, Alfred M.	1819	William Johnstone White	1828
Hughes, Charles	1825	William Barnard	1832
Hughes, William N.	1802	John Whittingham	1813
Humphreys, Thomas	1786	Joseph Round	1793
Jackson, Walter	1793	John Thompson	1801
Jackson, William R.	1846	George Mills	1868
Jenkins, James W.[1]	1870	James Faraday Barnard	1877
Kealy, Charles	1827	Alex. Walkinshaw	1837
Kemp, George	1806	Henry May	1813
Kemp, James	1813	George Kemp	1821
Kemp, Samuel	1785	John Fielding	1793
Knight, William	1805	Walter Jackson	1824
Lacy, George F.	1858	Samuel Jackson	1865
Lane, James	1789	John Thompson	1805

Appendix II

Apprentice	Bound	Master	Free
Lawes, —	1765	John Fielding	1773
Life, William	1772	William Innes	1780
Lloyd, William	1778	Hugh Clark	1786
Lockington, George	1838	Thomas Dowling	1846
Lovell, James	1807	Joseph Beckwith	1824
Luffman, Richard	1766	John Bayly	1773
Lyon, Joseph	1824	Alex. Findlay	1831
Martin, Henry	1811	John C. Russell	1829
Matthias, John	1821	Robert Oliver	1829
Mayfield, Thomas	1772	John Egerton	1779
Metcalf, John	1788	John Warner	1795
Middleton, Alfred	1874	George F. Lacy	1881
Midlane, John	1786	{ Charles Stevenson { William Bawtree	1793
Miles, William	1856	George D. Brome	1863
Mills, George	1807	Alex. Walkinshaw	1825
Mills, James D.	1839	Father (George)	1847
Mills, Joseph	1784	John Thompson	1817
Mumford, Jeremiah	1792	Robert Hennell III	1800
Moore, George	1825	William N. Hughes	1833
Nalder, George	1777	John Thompson	1781
Newman, Henry	1818	Gilbert J. Pickett	1826
Norris, William	1772	Father (William)	1780
Noyes, Edward	1766	William Clark	1773
Oliver, Robert	1808	Walter Jackson	1815
Ord, John	1778	Henry Gretton	1790
Orpin, James	1771	Mother (Ann)	1778
Osborne, Bartholomew E.	1890	John Beckwith	1897
Parsons, James	1827	Charles Mullens	1834
Peckham, George	1813	Henry Cooper	1821
Pescod, James[1]	1864	James Faraday Barnard	1871
Pickett, William J.	1801	Alex. Walkinshaw	1808
Press, Edward T.	1854	H. T. Trappett	1861
Price, John T.	1803	William Palmer	1810
Pritchard, William M.	1781	John Thompson	1789
Radclyffe, Thomas	1803	John P. Elven	1811
Radford, James	1815	Alex. Walkinshaw	1822
Rance, Henry	1822	Alex. Walkinshaw	1830
Ricordon, George M.	1840	John Rumley	1852

Appendix II

Apprentice	Bound	Master	Free
Roberts, John	1773	James Coly	1780
Roberts, John	1782	John Whittingham	1789
Roberts, Joseph	1806	Father	1814
Roberts, William J.	1862	John Foskett	1869
Robins, George E.	1806	Alex. Walkinshaw	1813
Robinson, William	1842	H. Hannaford	1850
Rogers, Ralph	1762	James Coly	1775
Rowe, Robert	1789	William Palmer	1796
Rumley, John	1815	Robert Oliver	1825
Russell, John C.	1787	Father (Charles)	1795
Seare, Thomas	1831	Father	1842
Shallis, James	1803	Joseph Beckwith	1810
Sherborn, Charles W.	1845	Robert Oliver	1852
Shove, John	1821	Charles Mullens	1828
Simpson, Richard	1772	William Palmer	1779
Slaughter, William J.	1870	William J. Roberts	1877
Smith, Charles	1884	T. E. Whittaker	1891
Smith, John W.	1810	William Moody	1810
Smith, William	1768	Butler Clowes	1775
Smith, William	1835	R. J. Augustus Edwards	1845
Snape, Charles E.	1881	G. F. Lacy	1889
Stanbury, Benjamin	1830	Charles Mullens	1830
Stevenson, Charles E.	1768	H. Copeland	1785
Steward, William A.[1]	1880	James Faraday Barnard	1888
Tanner, Edmund	1853	William R. Hearse	1860
Taylor, Henry	1770	Elizabeth widow of H. Copeland	1778
Tempest, Thomas	1805	William Norris	1812
Temple, George	1840	Samuel Jackson	1873
Thielcke, Henry D.	1802	Walter Jackson	1810
Thompson, Richard	1820	Father (Richard)	1827
Thornborough, Francis	1783	{ Henry May { James B. May	1797
Tompson, William M.	1820	Robert Oliver	1828
Torry, John T.	1861	James Faraday Barnard	1868
Toyne, William	1827	{ H. B. Hobdell { John Matthews	1835
Trimlett, Thomas	1782	George Bude	1813
Tuck, John	1861	William A. Shepherd	1869

Appendix II

Apprentice	Bound	Master	Free
Vincent, A. J.	1884	James Pescod	1891
Walkinshaw, Alex.	1784	W. Innes	1795
Waple, Illedge	1802	Alex. Adams	1810
Weedon, John	1815	Walter Jackson	1822
Weemys, David	1858	Walter Angell	1866
Weldon, Robert	1775	Elizabeth widow of Henry Copeland	1783
Westell, Richard	1777	John Thompson	1786
Whitfield, Thomas	1791	Thomas Mayfield	1798
Whittingham, John	1771	James Coly	1778
Williamson, Joseph	1761	Luke Kendall	1769
Williamson, Joseph	1781	John Warner	1789
Willson, George S.	1811	Gilbert J. Pickett	1819
Wincott, Thomas	1835	John Rumley	1842
Woodward, Henry	1783	John Thompson	1797
Wooley, Edward M.	1785	John Warner	1806
Wragg, Joseph B.	1799	George Bude	1807
Wright, Edward	1770	John Fielding	1781
Wrugglesworth, John	1835	Samuel Everingham	1843
Wyld, John D.	1789	Thomas Robinson	1797
Wyld, Matthew	1801	Thomas Robinson	1808

To this list of names may be added the following which are taken from the plaques upon the cases for the Westminster tobacco-box: 1815 J. Swaine; 1836 Page, Marsham St.; 1840 W. King, 25 Gt. Peter St. West^r.; 1853 King and Bowling of West^r.; 1878 and 1880 W. Scrivener.

Notes

1. Apprenticed to learn heraldic engraving.
2. An apprentice who became free by 'patrimony' did not have to go through the formality of being bound to his father.

Short Bibliography

Thomas Bewick, *Memoir of Thomas Bewick, written by himself 1822–1828*, 1961, reprint

Michael Clayton, *Collector's Dictionary of Silver and Gold of Great Britain and America*, 1971

A. J. Collins, *Jewels and Plate of Queen Elizabeth I*, 1955

J. M. Fritz, *Gestochene Bilder, Gravierungen auf deutschen Goldschmiederarbeiten der Spätgotik*, 1966

Arthur Grimwade, *Rococo Silver, 1727–1765*, 1974

H. Guilmard, *Les Maitres Ornamentistes*, 1880

Hanns Hammelmann, *Book Illustrations of the Eighteenth Century in England*, 1975

J. F. Hayward, *Huguenot Silver in England, 1688–1727*, 1959

A. M. Hind, *Engraving in England in the Sixteenth and Seventeenth Centuries*, I, 1952; II, 1955

A. M. Hind, Margery Corbett and Michael Norton, *The Reign of Charles I*, III, 1964

Edward Hodnett, *English Woodcuts, 1480–1535*, 1973

Randle Holme, *Academy of Armory and Blazon*, 1688

John Ireland and John Nichols, *Hogarth's Works*, 3 Vols., 1883

E. Alfred Jones, *Catalogue of the Collection of Old Plate of William Farrer*, 1924

John Nichols, *Biographical Anecdotes of William Hogarth*, 1781

Ronald Paulson, *Hogarth's Graphic Works*, 1965

Ronald Paulson, *Hogarth; his Life and Times*, 1971

T. F. Reddaway and E. M. Walker, *Early History of the Goldsmiths' Company, 1327–1509*, 1975

C. D. Sherborn, *A Sketch of the Life and Works of Charles William Sherborn*, 1912

Horace Walpole, *Anecdotes of Painting in England*, 1871 (reprint of 1786 edition)

Peter Winckworth, *The Westminster Tobacco-box*, 1966 (privately printed)

Index

Index

Index

Index